Strategic Planning for Law Firms:
A Practical Roadmap

2nd edition

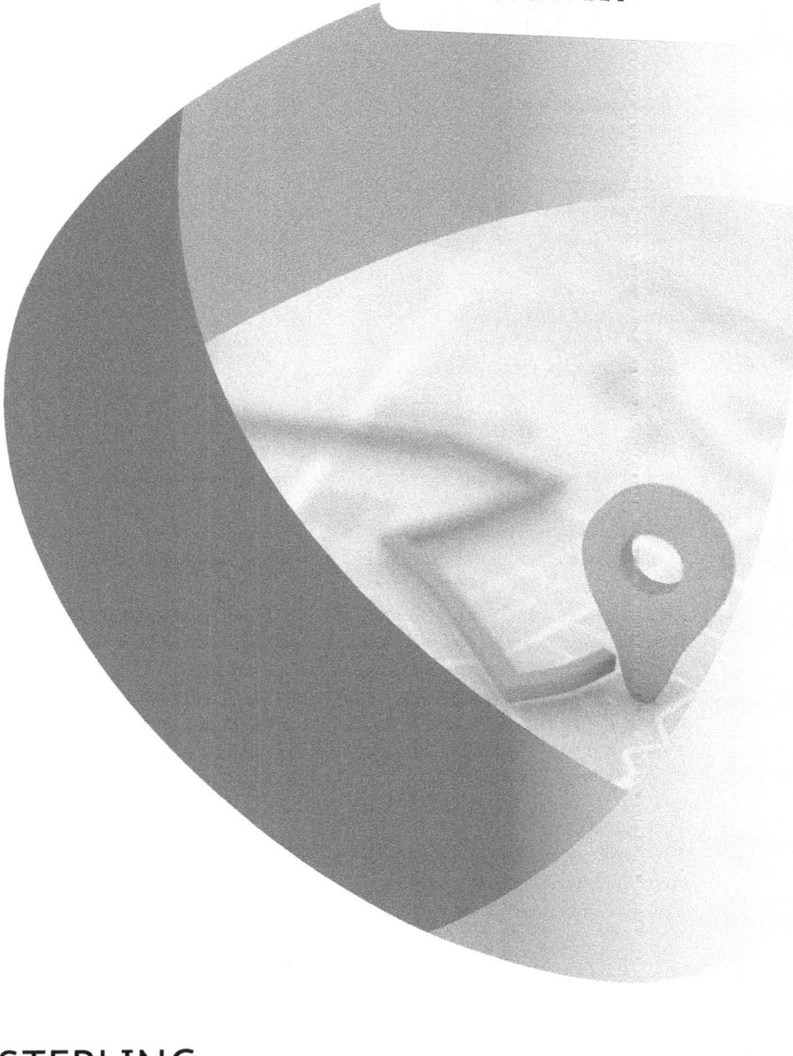

JOHN STERLING

Commissioning editor
Alex Davies

Editorial assistant
Francesca Ramadan

Published by
Globe Law and Business Ltd
3 Mylor Close
Horsell
Woking
Surrey GU21 4DD
United Kingdom
Tel: +44 20 3745 4770
www.globelawandbusiness.com

ISBN: 978-1-78358-356-0
A catalogue record for this book is available from the British Library

Contents

Executive summary vii

About the author xiii

Chapter 1: Strategic planning process overview 1
  Phase I – Situation analysis 1
  Phase II – Direction setting 2
  Phase III – Strategy and objective development 2
  Phase IV – Implementation planning 2

Chapter 2: Phase I – Situation analysis 5
  Internal analysis 6
  External analyses 18
  Strategic issues 22

Chapter 3: Phase II – Setting strategic direction 25
  Vision 25
  Mission 28
  Primary excellence goals 32
  Process design – developing strategic direction 35
  Further reading 39

Chapter 4: Phase III – Strategy development 41
  Strategy development 41
  Strategic thinking 41
  Strategy development – trade-offs and choices 44
  Practice portfolio management 45
  Format for strategies 46
  Objective development 47
  A final caveat regarding objectives 47

Chapter 5: Phase IV – Implementation planning 49
Action planning approach..49
Balanced scorecard approach 53
Balanced scorecard principles 53

Chapter 6: Strategic issues – universal challenges to be addressed in the context of law firm strategic planning 57
Talent management...57
Client expectations for value 61
Profit growth and financial management 66
Succession planning and management..................................72
Information management 74
Disaggregation of legal processes 76
Business development and marketing..................................78

Chapter 7: Strategic planning tools and principles 83
1. Portfolio analysis 83
2. Product life cycle management 90
3. Competitive intensity – five forces analysis.....................94
4. Scenario-based planning 97
5. Balanced scorecard..100

Chapter 8: Value innovation tools and techniques 105
Disruptive innovation 106
Co-creating unique value with customers 110
Blue ocean strategy 112
Business model canvas..117

Case study 1: Intellectual property boutique, efficient director involvement – Sterne, Kessler, Goldstein and Fox.......................................121
Preparation and process design.....................................121
Fact-gathering and background analysis.............................122
Direction setting and strategy development 122
Implementation planning and closure 123
Update...124
Implementation and results from initial strategy 124
Strategy updates and looking forward 126

Case study 2: Mid-size firm, governance driven process – Clark Hill...... 129
Preparation and process objectives 129

Fact gathering and background analysis 130
Strategic planning 131
Implementation planning 131
Closure and member retreat 132
Update 132
Developments at the firm 132
Subsequent strategic planning 133
Leadership insights (hindsight is 20/20) 134

Case study 3: Big firm, broad involvement – Bryan Cave Leighton Paisner 135
Initial preparation 135
Fact gathering and background development 136
Direction setting workshop 137
Wharton Insights 138
Strategy development 138
Exposure, feedback and refinement 139
Implementation planning 139
Adoption and formal roll-out 140
Update 140
Developments at the firm 141
Subsequent strategic planning processes 141
Leadership insights (hindsight is 20/20) 142

Executive summary

At its core, the purpose of strategy in any for-profit organization is to position the firm to achieve better and more sustainable returns than the competition. In other words, the purpose of strategy is to capture a sustainable competitive advantage. Doing so requires the firm to satisfy major stakeholders (primarily customers, but also knowledge workers, shareholders, and others) over both the near and longer term. Ultimately, business strategy is about winning in competitive markets.

The origins of business strategy can be traced to the immediate post-WWII era and Peter Drucker's 1946 book, *Concepts of the Corporation*. Drucker gets to the heart of the issue, making the following point:

> *"A company's primary responsibility is to serve its customers. Profit is not the primary goal, but rather an essential condition for the company's continued existence. There is only one valid definition of business purpose: to create a customer."*

In other words, if an organization cannot satisfy its clients in a superior manner over a sustained period, the rest of its mission is doomed – there will be no profits for the shareholders, no wages for the workforce, and no future for the firm.

Business strategy really began to flower in the 1960s, when Bruce Henderson founded the Boston Consulting Group (BCG). Other consultancies already existed, but BCG cemented the idea of business strategy. The premise that tools and models could directly influence business performance gained legitimacy during this period. Firms like BCG, Bain & Company, McKinsey & Company, and Arthur D. Little all contributed to the proliferation of useful models and tools. Thus, today most managers understand things like economies of scale and the experience curve, product life cycles, and the various matrices that consultants trot out to analyze markets and businesses (many of the most pertinent tools and models for law firms are covered in-depth in this book).

More than perhaps any consultant, academic, or management guru, Michael Porter has provided the central definitions for what we know today as business strategy and strategic planning. In his seminal 1985 book, *Competitive Advantage: Creating and Sustaining Superior Performance*, Porter began with the supposition that "Competition is at the core of the success or failure of firms... Competitive strategy aims to establish a profitable and sustainable position against the forces that determine industry competition."

Porter highlighted three so-called generic strategies in *Competitive Advantage*:

1. Cost leadership (i.e. capturing customers on the basis of price);
2. Differentiation (i.e. capturing customers on the basis of offering unique value); and
3. Focus (i.e. targeting narrow markets in which your firm has an advantage).

A decade or so later, he refined this thinking. Specifically, Porter's landmark *Harvard Business Review* article entitled "What is Strategy?" sharpened the definition. Specifically he noted:

> *"Competitive strategy is about being different. It means deliberately choosing a different set of activities to deliver a unique mix of value."*

Porter makes the further point that simply pursuing the low cost position is not a source of sustainable advantage – someone is always willing to go lower. In the legal marketplace we see this manifest in many ways – the continual erosion of rates and margins in insurance defense, the increased disaggregation of legal projects and the related rise of alternative legal service providers, and the standardization of transactional and other documents (e.g. simple wills, loan documents, etc.).

The increasing competitiveness of the legal industry – both for people and for clients – has led some to look for so-called "blue oceans". W. Chan Kim and Renée Mauborgne, professors at INSEAD, analyzed strategies across hundreds of organizations and described an approach to strategy that focused on pursuing uncontested markets (i.e. blue oceans), rather than deeply competitive markets (i.e. red oceans). Others have turned to business model innovation, using Alexander Osterwalder's *Business Model Canvas* both to scrutinize existing business models and to create business models for ancillary businesses and/or novel practice areas. Discussion of both Blue Ocean Strategy and the Business Model Canvas are new in this edition.

Theory and history are all well and good, but how does this really translate in a law firm environment? This report provides readers with a solid grounding in the key elements of a strategic plan (which apply both at the firm and at the practice group level). Namely, a well constructed strategic plan includes:

- A concise and compelling vision and mission;
- A well articulated and focused set of primary goals;
- Strategies that allocate resources toward achieving those goals; and
- Related implementation plans that prioritize near term action and highlight meaningful measures and milestones that track implementation.

Further, this report provides the reader with a workable, real world strategic planning process they can use in their own firms. That process includes:

- An approach to developing a strong analytical foundation and framework – providing an objective, factual assessment of the internal and external environment facing the firm;
- A means of defining the firm's strategic direction – enabling the firm to articulate and agree upon its direction including:
  - What the firm (or practice group) aspires to become over the long run; and
  - What position(s) the firm or practice intends to occupy (i e. what it will be known for).
- A means of developing action oriented strategies – enabling the firm (or practice) to agree upon the sometimes difficult trade-offs among its strategic alternatives, enabling it to focus resources on achieving its aspirations and desired market positions; and
- An approach for identifying near term action plans (and prioritizing those action plans) so that individuals are directly engaged in (and are accountable for) roles that put the strategy into operation on a day-to-day basis.

Readers will find the remainder of this book organized into the following major sections:

- **A strategic planning process roadmap** – providing a detailed guide to best practices for strategy development and strategic planning in a law firm context;
- **An expanded review of strategic management tools and principles** – providing a pragmatic overview of the most important and useful analytical tools and strategic management principles that drive winning strategies for law firms, including:
  - Portfolio analysis tools and techniques;
  - Product/service life cycle management;
  - Competitive intensity analyses (the so-called five forces);
  - Scenario planning techniques;
  - Disruptive innovation principles;
  - Co-creation principles;
  - Blue Ocean strategy development;
  - Business model canvas; and
  - Balanced scorecard tools.
- **A discussion of strategic issues facing law firms** – providing a guide to the universal challenges and question law firms face in the context of strategic planning, including:
  - People issues;
  - Knowledge management;
  - Project management;
  - Value drivers and pricing (fees in the context of client relationships);
  - Profitability and financial management;
  - Succession management; and
  - Outsourcing and smart-sourcing.
- **Case studies** – highlighting real world examples of how the process has worked in large, mid-size and boutique law firms – updated to reflect how firms are coping strategically with the post-crash, flat demand environment we have seen over the past five years.

Readers of the previous edition will find much new to explore in the second edition, including a thoroughly updated discussion of the core strategic issues facing law firms; refreshed case studies that outline real world responses to current strategic issues, strategic planning challenges, and strategy implementation imperatives; a deep dive into applying "Blue Ocean" strategy in a law firm setting; and a discussion of how the "Business Model Canvas" can be used to rethink practice areas, pricing, and ancillary businesses.

About the author

John Sterling is chief marketing officer at Sterne Kessler Goldstein & Fox, a leading IP specialty firm based in Washington, DC. He is also the founding partner of Sterling Strategies, LLC. Prior to founding Sterling Strategies, John was a founding partner at Smock Sterling Strategic Management Consultants. He has over 30 years of experience in strategic management and market research.

John has worked extensively with law and other professional service firms, as well as with industrial and consumer product companies and not-for-profit organisations.

His work with TimeLine Theatre Company in Chicago won the Richard Goodman Strategic Planning Award for excellence in strategic planning from the Association for Strategic Planning.

John is past president of the Strategic Management Association in Chicago and is a contributing editor to the business journal *Strategy & Leadership*.

Chapter 1:
Strategic planning process overview

This chapter provides a detailed roadmap for creating a strategic plan at the firm or practice group level – assuming one is starting essentially with a blank sheet of paper. Note that in many instances (perhaps most instances today), firms are not starting with a totally blank slate. Many firms will start the planning process with a well-considered and widely embraced mission and/or with a clearly understood set of shared cultural values.

This chapter describes a four-phased process for strategic planning – as depicted in Figure 1 and broadly outlined in the following points. In general, the process works from the bigger picture and the longer term and moves gradually toward more specific decisions and the nearer term.

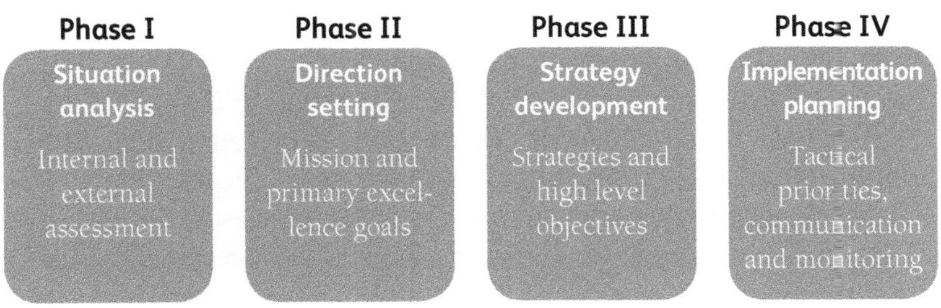

Figure 1: The schematic phased process for creating a strategic plan.

Phase I – Situation analysis

The situation analysis phase is designed to ensure strategy development is built on a foundation of facts. The intent is to avoid so-called "analysis paralysis", while establishing a shared understanding of the internal state of the firm (or practice) and the external, competitive market environment it faces. Ideally, work during this phase is driven by a principle of information sufficiency (i.e. gathering enough information and performing enough analysis to understand the situation). Frankly, there is always one more data point that could be gathered, but ultimately continual fact gathering will result in diminishing returns.

Phase II – Direction setting

The direction setting phase focuses on reaching agreement on the big picture questions. What does the firm (or practice) aspire to become? What will it focus resources on to gain a sustained competitive advantage? The end product is generally some combination of a well-articulated vision and mission for the firm (or practice) and a related set of primary goals. The time horizon in the direction setting phase is longer term – three to five years (often longer with regard to the vision).

Phase III – Strategy and objective development

The strategy development phase focuses on making strategic trade-offs among rational alternatives. Since resources are necessarily limited – in a law firm environment, time is the most finite resource – choices need to be made. The strategy development phase enables the firm (or practice) to answer the question, "What do we intend to do to achieve our primary goals?" The issue of how (in the very near term) the firm will implement those decisions is a matter for Phase IV. In addition, this phase positions the firm to identify high level measurable objectives that will enable management to assess progress against the primary goals – answering the fundamental question, "Are the strategies working/ helping us to achieve our goals?"

Phase IV – Implementation planning

This final phase puts the strategic plan into action in the near term. At the firm level, it should enable the practices, firm leadership, and firm administration to align activities with the strategic direction of the firm. Further, it prioritizes action, so that efforts are not wasted or dissipated. At the practice group level, it creates clear roles and responsibilities for every member of the group – so that everyone is engaged in some meaningful way in the implementation of the strategy.

There has been considerable debate – in the strategy literature and among strategy professionals – surrounding the subject of "top down versus bottom up" approaches to strategic planning. The process detailed in the following sections makes that debate largely irrelevant. The process needs to be both top down and bottom up.

Critically, people need to be engaged early in the process to think (and opine) on the state of the law firm (or practice) and the opportunities and threats apparent in the external market. Further, people should be engaged from the outset in thinking about and talking about the long-term direction and vision the firm should pursue.

Likewise, people need to have a direct understanding of what the resulting strategic plan means for them on both a near and long-term basis. Ideally, they should have some direct role in moving the firm (or at the very least, their practice group or team) in the direction the partners have agreed to go.

To further aid bottom-up engagement, process check-points can be created to share working drafts with all but the largest partnerships as the planning process unfolds. Thus, the process should have a bottom up character both at the beginning and the end of the process and can include even more involvement if that is desirable.

That said, with the exception of very small firms, a smaller group will need to do some of the heavier lifting associated with articulating the strategic direction, working through strategic trade-offs and choices, and setting high level objectives. There are many ways to engage a broader (even a very large) partnership in adjusting and affirming those decisions. However, some smaller group will need to take the lead – and there are many ways to make that work effectively (see the case studies at the end of this book for some real-world examples). Some alternatives include:

- Working directly through the governance structure of the firm – using the firm's management committee, board of directors, or executive committee (or their counterparts) to act as the de facto strategic planning committee;
- Creating an ad hoc strategic planning committee broadly representative of the partnership vis-à-vis areas of practice and thought leadership. With highly capable process facilitation, an ad hoc committee of this nature can be relatively large (roughly 25 members). While that may not satisfy every political consideration in the partnership, it should enable even fairly large partnerships to be well represented; and
- Engaging in a hybrid approach in which a small governance body (e.g. an executive committee) develops draft work products at each stage of the process and a larger committee engages in debate and discussion to improve upon those drafts – freeing the large group from getting bogged down in "wordsmithing", but enabling that large group to be directly involved in strategy development.

This overview underscores the need for good process design, management, and facilitation. That in turn raises a recurring question. Does a firm need an outside consultant in order to develop a strategic plan? The short answer is no. Many firms develop strategic plans without outside assistance and that includes some of the most successful law firms in the world.

A broader question is, how and where can consultants add value to a firm's efforts? A good consultant should be able to tailor a planning process so that it fits the firm well – leveraging the right analytical models and applying the right strategic principles to the issues facing the firm. A good consultant should bring strong facilitation (and listening) skills to the process – to ensure partners' time is used efficiently and effectively throughout the process. Finally, a good consultant should balance industry expertise and knowledge with creativity and an open mind – ensuring the firm avoids pitfalls and blind alleys, while encouraging the firm to find its strategic differences (rather than forcing law firm management dogma on the firm's leadership team).

The following four chapters provide a more detailed discussion of each phase of the strategic planning process. Each chapter includes a description of the substantive work products that should emerge from the respective phase, a guideline for structuring and managing that phase, and tips and tools that may be useful to individual readers as they pursue the process.

Chapter 2:
Phase I – Situation analysis

The situation analysis phase is designed to ensure strategy development is built on a factual understanding of the internal and external environment facing the firm or practice group. The goal of this phase is to establish a shared understanding (at a minimum among those charged with drafting the strategic plan, but ideally among all partners) of the internal state of the firm (or practice) and the external, competitive market environment it faces. Ideally, work during this phase is driven by a principle of information sufficiency (i.e. gathering enough information and performing enough analysis to understand the situation).

There are two primary risks in the situation analysis phase and in many respects they are counterpoints to one another. The first risk involves rushing through (or even skipping) situation analysis – leading the strategy development process to yield "factless focus". This risk is significant in a law firm environment for a number of reasons:

- First, firms and practice groups are led by extraordinarily smart and well-educated people – creating the temptation to assume the situation is already well understood from the outset;
- Second, some of the background information gathering and analysis can be uncomfortable (at least for some partners):
    - Objective analysis of financial performance – especially across practice groups – can be divisive;
    - Asking clients for candid feedback and forward-looking advice makes some partners uncomfortable for a variety of reasons (e.g. fear of negative feedback, concern that they will not be able to follow-though on client suggestions, concern that someone else is talking to "my client", and the list goes on); and
    - Analysis of practice capabilities and/or the relative attractiveness of selected legal markets will inevitably highlight weaknesses or

external threats some would prefer to ignore ("whistling past the (proverbial) graveyard").

- Third, information gathering and analysis requires time and other resources – and time in particular is a precious commodity in a law firm environment.

The parallel risk in this phase is falling victim to paralysis by analysis. Frankly, there is always one more data point that could be gathered and one more analytical model that could be applied to that data. Ultimately, incremental fact gathering and analysis will experience diminishing returns. The analogy that seems most apt for the situation analysis phase is to view it as a jigsaw puzzle – at some point the picture becomes clear, well before the last pieces are put into the puzzle. Stop when there is broad understanding of the situation, not when every possible question has been asked and answered.

The situation analysis phase involves two broad components – internal analyses and external analyses. Each is discussed in some depth in the sections below.

Internal analysis

Internal analyses are intended to help a firm create an honest and objective understanding of its strengths, weaknesses, and organizational capabilities. While some situations may dictate additional internal analyses, most firms can focus on developing information from four sources of data: qualitative input from lawyers and administrative leaders; financial data; professional capability assessments; infrastructure and management capability reviews.

Qualitative input (from lawyers and administrative leaders)

As noted earlier, law firms and practice groups have the distinct advantage of being led by people of extraordinary intellect. They do know and understand a great deal about their practices, their clients, their capabilities and shortcomings, and the firm in general. While they should not be the sole source of information and analysis about the situation facing the firm (or practice), they should be an important early source.

Asking the partners (or in most cases all attorneys and senior administrators) for their views regarding firm (or practice) strengths and weaknesses, external opportunities and challenges, important strategic issues to be addressed, and their respective initial vision for the future of the firm, is a very productive first step:

- It surfaces ideas and issues very early in the process;
- It provides useful guidance for other analyses (i.e. it highlights issues and concerns to consider and examine); and
- Perhaps most importantly, it provides a means of front-end involvement in the planning process for a critical stakeholder group. This early involvement helps to build both widespread understanding of the situation and ultimate agreement and buy-in to the strategies that emerge later in the process.

From a process design standpoint, the most efficient way to gather input from attorneys and other firm leaders is via survey. This is particularly true in firms with more than 100 attorneys. However, surveys can be cold and highly generic if they are simply pulled off the shelf (or from an article suggesting "20 Questions You Should Ask Your Partners"). The following approach can help readers to develop a highly relevant and customized survey.

First, interview a cross-section of thought leaders (e.g. members of the governing committee(s) and/or ad hoc planning committee, practice area leaders, etc.) via a combination of one-on-one and small group sessions. Use the following topics as a broad guide for those interviews and focus groups.

- What is the current state of the firm?
- What are our greatest strengths as a firm? What are our strongest practices?
- What are our most vexing weaknesses? Which practices are weakest and/or facing important capability gaps?
- What external trends in the legal marketplace should we be addressing – either because they create tremendous opportunities for us or because they represent significant threats to our firm and our business model?
- What strategic issues do we need to confront as a law firm? What are the major trade-offs we face and what reasonable alternatives do we have relative to those trade-offs?
- If things go well over the next five years, what should this firm look like (e.g. scope of services, size, market position, geographic footprint, culture, etc.)?

After 15-20 interviews, clear patterns will emerge from these interviews and small group discussions. Use the points that recur to craft a parallel set of closed ended questions for each of the topics above. In other words, create a survey that enables the firm's attorneys and administrative leaders to react to the recurring themes the thought leaders identified in the following areas.

- The firm's core strengths and weaknesses should be explored:
  - Lists of strengths and weaknesses can be easily honed from the interviews;
  - Attorneys and administrative leaders can be asked to rate each strength/weakness on a scale (e.g. from "not an important strength" to "major strength upon which we should build"); and
  - Wording for the question itself can be fairly simple. For instance, "Please rate each of the following strengths of our firm relative to your agreement that each is a substantial strength upon which to build for the future."
- Market opportunities and challenges or threats likewise should be explored:
  - Similarly, the lists of external opportunities and threats can be honed from the thought leader interviews (and the process leader's own understanding of the external marketplace);
  - Similar rating scales should be crafted to enable attorneys and other leaders to rate external opportunities and threats; and
  - Sample wording for the questions in this area would be, "Please rate the following external threats to our firm and its market position."
- It is often productive to simply ask everyone in the firm to rate the relative market position of each major practice team, as well as the future growth potential of each practice. This involves two parallel questions:
  - "Please share your opinion regarding the relative market position (in our city/region/etc.) of the firm's major practice areas." The rating scale for this question should likely include four or more choices including, "Clear leader in market share and substance"; "Among the leaders, but at parity with one or more other high-quality practices"; "Well respected, but trailing

other market leaders"; and "Clearly lagging other practices in the city/region/nation."

- "Which of our practice areas have the greatest opportunities to grow profitable revenues over the next few years (please rate the growth prospects of each practice below in the context of their respective external market prospects)?" The rating scale for this question can be simple – "Strong growth prospects", "Modest growth prospects", "Weak growth prospects."

• Questions regarding strategic trade-offs can be structured as a series of choices on a bi-polar scale or as a list of issues to be rated.

- An example of a bi-polar scale set of strategic trade-offs would include a question like, "If forced to make a strategic trade-off between the choices on either end of the following scales, I would rather see our firm (please select one point/box along each trade-off continuum)" – with a customized set of trade-offs like the examples listed in the table below.

Make centralized decisions on investments intended to grow the most profitable practices	☐	☐	☐	☐	☐	Empower entrepreneurial lawyers to grow practice areas without regard to centralized/firm priorities
Ensuring practice diversity/full service capabilities	☐	☐	☐	☐	☐	Ensuring growth in our most dynamic practice areas
Creating a comfortable work environment	☐	☐	☐	☐	☐	Maximizing per partner profitability

- A simpler approach involves listing the major strategic issues facing the firm and asking attorneys and administrative leaders to rate the relative importance of a list of strategic issues honed from the thought leader interviews – for instance, "The firm faces a range of strategic and tactical issues as it begins this planning process. Please rate the following list of strategic issues in terms of their relative importance to the future of our law firm."

- Attorneys and administrative leaders can also rate a list of shared values identified by thought leaders, as well as potential points that could/should be included in the firm's vision for the future (e.g. rating their relative level of agreement with a series of phrases or statements regarding the future of the law firm).

Include an area for open-ended responses at the end of each question. If the closed-ended questions are well designed, most attorneys will not feel the need to share additional comments. However, it is both professionally courteous and potentially valuable to provide that opportunity for open-ended commentary.

There are numerous online tools that are free or nearly free that will enable the firm to host the survey online – providing a degree of anonymity for respondents (which is particularly helpful vis-à-vis gaining honest input from more junior people). If more refined analysis of survey input is desirable, ask a few demographic questions at the end of the survey to enable logical breakdowns of the data (e.g. partner/associate/administration, practice group, etc.).

This baseline input provides a helpful qualitative source of information that will be useful throughout the process – including the balance of the situation analysis phase.

Financial performance

Historical financial performance is an obvious focal point for background analysis. Most firms today have robust accounting and financial systems that enable creative and in-depth financial analysis. For strategic planning purposes, the key trends and statistics to analyze involve revenues and margins (or profitability).

Analysis can and should be performed at a number of levels as a means of gaining factual insights into the financial position and potential of the firm and/or practice. Namely, financial analysis should examine performance at the firm level, at the practice area level, at the client level, and at the individual partner or attorney level. Different insights are gained from each set of analyses.

Firm level statistics

Firm level statistics and trends are familiar to most readers – firms generally produce regular reports on firm level financial performance and many partners are adept at translating the implications of those firm level statistics to their personal expectations. Among the strategic planning related questions to consider in the context of firm level statistics are the following:

- What direction have revenues been heading over the past five years – overall as well as on a per attorney, per partner, and per equity partner basis? Are the revenue ratios disguising important underlying trends (e.g. has the firm been managing the denominator of the ratios to keep the partners happy, while the underlying revenue trends are more sobering)?
- Similarly, what direction are overall margins heading? If published profitability statistics have taught us anything over the past 20 years, it is that profitability ratios (e.g. profits per equity partner) are subject to manipulation. Analysis of overall margins can remove some of that statistical noise and distortion to help inform the strategic planning process.
- Are there important balance sheet statistics or trends that could have a substantial influence on strategic planning? For instance:
    - Are debt levels rising, falling, remaining stable;
    - Are retirement obligations well-funded; and
    - Are there unusual liabilities or assets on the balance sheet that could influence the firm's ability to follow through on its strategy?

Practice level statistics

Practice level statistics and trends can be more difficult to obtain for a variety of reasons. First, many attorneys work across more than one practice group – how should both the costs and revenues of those people be accounted for in practice level statistics? Second, many firms are understandably reluctant to produce practice level margin analyses due to the potentially divisive nature of such statistics. Third, a meaningful portion of overhead is not easily allocated to practices (e.g. accounting department, information services department, and similar costs).

For purposes of strategic planning, the important statistics and trends can be boiled down to two areas – revenues and contribution to profit.

- Revenues are a straightforward prospect for most practices. The only potential ambiguity involves tracking revenues associated with individuals working across practices. Often, that ambiguity can be cleared up via matter level tracking (i.e. regardless of who works on a matter, it is generally coded to a particular practice area). When in doubt, designate primary practices for each time keeper and force revenue to follow the person.

- Contribution to profit is an approach to tracking practice level profitability that eliminates the ambiguity associated with allocating indirect expenses. Assuming each practice's revenues are a function of the dollars collected on the efforts of fee earners designated as members of that practice, contribution simply backs out the direct costs associated with generating that revenue.

	Year 1	Year 2	Year 3	Year 4
Revenues				
Gross billings by fee earners				
Less discounts				
Less write-offs				
Net billings by fee earners				
Direct expenses				
Salaries/draws of fee earners and support staff				
Benefit costs for fee earners and support staff				
Occupancy costs for fee earners and support staff				
Direct marketing expenditures				
Direct library/research expenditures				

- Contribution is a function of the net billings of all fee earners in the group, less the direct expenses that are clearly attributed to those fee earners (e.g. salaries, benefits, direct support staff, marketing and business development spending, research and reference costs, etc.).

While it can be tempting to focus primarily on differences across practices (e.g. on the relative contribution to profit of each group), that focus only provides limited insight. Certainly, it is important to understand which practices are more or less profitable on a contribution basis. That understanding can help to validate (or invalidate) the input attorneys and others offered in the qualitative survey for instance.

However, that focus needs to be augmented by a meaningful analysis of underlying trends relative to gross production, realization drivers (e.g. discounts and write-offs), the direct costs associated with partners and other fee earners, and other aspects of contribution. That analysis may reveal strengths and weaknesses that transcend individual practices (for instance, a systemic inclination to discounting).

In other words, practice level analysis provides important insights regarding the relative strengths and weaknesses across the firm's practices (vis-à-vis financial performance), but it also reveals important recurring trends that illuminate strengths and weaknesses associated with firm level strategic or philosophical approaches to practice management.

Client level financial analyses

Client level financial analyses should include a number of considerations. Critically, is the firm overly dependent on one or a few clients for a substantial portion of its revenues? It is not unusual to see one or a few clients representing a large share of the revenues in a small firm. However, mid-size and larger firms that are heavily dependent on one or a few clients should consider this revenue concentration to be a material strategic issue.

Conversely, is the firm earning a substantial portion of its revenues from very small clients and/or matters? This may be entirely appropriate for some practices (e.g. an estate planning boutique that handles many small matters for individual clients every year). However, in a diversified mid-sized or larger firm, a large number of small clients and matters may highlight a risk of future conflicts.

Are particular clients (or more importantly, particular classes of clients) exhibiting discernible financial trends? For instance, are certain classes of clients exhibiting higher or lower realization ratios? Likewise, are certain clients or classes of clients becoming a growing or declining portion of firm revenues?

Finally, does client level financial analysis highlight important industry expertise that spans practice groups? If so, is the firm actively pursuing that industry concentration and is the firm capitalizing on its depth within given industries?

Partner and/or attorney level financial analyses

Partner and/or attorney level financial analyses are also potentially revealing. Firms typically maintain detailed performance statistics for all attorneys – even in firms with lock-step or purely subjective compensation systems. Thus, statistics are often available regarding billable hours worked, total hours worked, revenues collected (or realized) from billable time worked, revenues collected (or realized) from clients originated by an attorney(s), revenues collected (or realized) from clients and/or matters managed by an attorney(s), revenues collected (or realized) from newly originated matters, etc.

At the partner level (both equity and non-equity), it is worthwhile correlating the objective performance statistics with actual compensation (e.g. draws, plus profit distributions, plus bonuses).

The primary insight gained from such a correlation or regression analysis is an understanding of what the firm is actually rewarding. Those rewards may or may not align effectively with what the firm expects and values from its partners. For instance, many firms intend to reward partners for developing, managing, and growing client relationships, but they actually reward billable hours and working attorney receipts heavily.

This analysis can also help to reveal what (if anything from a financial point of view) has driven promotion to partner in recent years.

Ultimately, financial analyses are a lesson in historical trends and should be considered in that context. There are valuable insights to be gained from looking objectively at financial trends and statistics. However, those insights need to be considered in the broader context of professional capabilities, client relationships, and broader external market trends.

Professional capabilities

The capabilities, productivity, and demographic profile of a firm's professional staff (particularly the partnership, but extending to all attorneys

and paraprofessionals) are important background considerations in preparing for long range or strategic planning. The following factors in particular lend themselves to analytical study.

- The demographic profile of the firm's and/or the practice's attorneys and key staff members is a critical consideration. The calendar will turn and there is no stopping the aging process. Thus, the firm's age profile is extremely predictable.
  - Significant gaps in the age and experience profile of the firm – and particularly within practice areas – is easy to spot and is a meaningful consideration when planning for the long run.
  - Likewise, the progression of the senior-most people toward anticipated (if not mandatory) retirement is an important planning consideration.
  - While planning for and managing client, knowledge, and practice succession is a sensitive subject, it cannot and should not be avoided in the planning process.
- Productivity statistics and trends can and likely should be juxtaposed against demographic profiles.
  - For instance, it is not only important to understand what substantive capability and knowledge gaps may be created by impending retirements. It is also important to understand how much productive economic contribution is at risk of being lost to retirement.
  - In part, this lost production is a simple function of the hours spent serving clients, extended by billing rates that are undoubtedly among the highest in the firm – given the level of experience and prestige senior attorneys bring to the table.
  - Critically, the retirement of senior partners also often carries with it the risk of diminished (or entirely lost) client relationships. Many senior partners are among the most successful business developers and relationship managers. Their retirements if not well orchestrated, create the risk of substantial revenue losses – far beyond the lost production of a single attorney's billable time.
- An unvarnished appraisal of demographics and production should also consider the potential for reasonably predictable career stage changes in attorneys' performance. For instance, while senior people often taper down their activity in their final years of practice,

a transactional attorney in his or her late 30s is likely just hitting stride as a business originator, and a litigator in his or her late 40s is probably only now beginning to be recognized by peers and potential clients as a "go to" person.

- More simply, a look across the professional ranks of the firm (or practice group) can reveal important gaps in service capabilities as well. For instance, analysis of professional capabilities can and should highlight gaps in substantive legal capabilities needed by clients.
  - This is obviously true for general service firms, which can often pinpoint a lack of depth in substantive areas.
  - It can be equally true in a boutique setting, where a gap in technical knowledge can hold back an intellectual property practice, or a thinness in trial experience can limit the long run prospects of a litigation boutique.
- Finally, when assessing professional capabilities, a review or management audit of the relative strengths and weaknesses of the firm's professional development and its recruiting programs is warranted as well.
  - The firm's ability to close some of the professional capability gaps via internal development will depend heavily on the strength of its professional development programs (both formal and informal).
  - Likewise, the firm's ability to close demographic and substantive legal capability gaps may depend entirely on the firm's ability to recruit both entry level law students, as well as experienced attorneys via lateral hiring.

Infrastructure and management capabilities

Finally, there are a number of management capabilities and back office infrastructure competencies that can strongly influence the strategic success or failure of the firm. Among the functional management capabilities that should be considered and assessed as part of internal analyses associated with strategic planning are the following:

- Information technology capabilities are increasingly important to the practice of law and to the management of the law firm as a business entity. Firms maintain a variety of systems and support capabilities. A simple question to ask relative to information technology platforms is, "Are our capabilities ahead of the market, at parity with the market, or lagging the market?" Among the systems capabilities to at least qualitatively review are:

- Document management systems;
- Litigation support systems and/or external vendor relationships (particularly with regard to electronic discovery capabilities);
- Analytical and productivity tools leveraging machine learning and artificial intelligence;
- Project management, work flow management, and collaboration support tools and platforms (including budget and alternative fee management capabilities);
- Desktop and mobile productivity tools and platforms streamlining daily tasks; and
- Financial and managerial decision support tools and platforms.

- A management review of the firm's marketing and business development capabilities is helpful in advance of strategic planning. The Legal Marketing Association[1] (North America) provides a body of knowledge covering core skills needed in marketing communications, advisory bulletins, and other resources that can guide a qualitative assessment of marketing capabilities at the firm and the practice group level.
  - Marketing and business development departments have grown and become more sophisticated in law firms. As a result, firms' and practices' expectations of what those departments can and should deliver have grown as well.
  - Clients are subscribing to (or maintaining their own) performance statistics on law firms – business development needs to be capable of providing similar analyses to client relationship managers so they are prepared to discuss performance with clients.
  - It is important to put your firm's assessment in the context of the level of resources the firm is investing in marketing and business development.
- Recruiting, professional development, and human resource management functions are often distinct from one another in a law firm setting. Regardless of how integrated (or not) a firm's talent management and people support functions are, it is important to

assess how effective those support functions are in the context of broader firm strengths and weaknesses. In the US, NALP[2] provides a range of tools and resources to help assess and improve recruiting and professional development – particularly at the entry and early career levels of law firms. Other organizations also conduct associate satisfaction surveys that rank law firms for prospective recruits (see The Vault[3] and Chambers Associate[4]).

- Some firms have formalized data science functions to build proprietary solutions that automate repetitive cognitive tasks. Many others have turned to service providers who provide data mining and analytical tools that support effective legal practice. That functional capability is becoming critical in selected areas of practice.
- Finally, many firms have formally invested in knowledge management capabilities. Some locate the function within the information technology department – viewing it primarily as a document governance management role. Others have larger scale investment in knowledge management – with a chief knowledge officer focused on integrating document management, professional development, succession planning and other knowledge centric considerations to gain a competitive advantage for the law firm. Again, assessment of this area should be done in the context of the level of investment the firm is making in knowledge management.

Ultimately, the goal of the internal assessment is to gain a meaningful and objective understanding of the firm's genuine strengths, weaknesses, and organizational capabilities. That understanding of the internal environment will help inform the strategic choices to be made in subsequent phases of the strategic planning process.

External analyses

External analyses are intended to help a firm to develop a reasoned understanding of its position in the competitive marketplace, as well as the primary opportunities and threats evident in the external environment. While some situations may dictate additional external research and analyses, most firms can focus on developing information from three areas of focus (plus a review of big picture or so-called "mega" trends): input and feedback from clients; peer group/peer firm comparisons; and practice group market area assessments. Each of these focus areas is discussed in more depth in the sections below.

Client feedback and input

In truth, firms and practice groups should be systematically gathering and responding to client input and feedback on a regular (if not continuous) basis. The term systematic is chosen deliberately to mean client feedback that is gathered via a consistent set of questions and that is analyzed in a centralized or actively managed manner.

If your firm does gather systematic client feedback on a regular basis, that existing client input may very well be sufficient for the purposes of ensuring client input informs the strategic planning process. A basic process for gathering sufficient client input for strategic planning purposes involves the following steps.

First, identify a solid cross-section of clients from whom informed and candid input can be gathered. Depending on the size of the firm (or practice group), the level of practice diversification in the firm, and the geographic scope of the firm, interviews with as few as 15 or as many as 50 clients may be required to obtain systematic insights for strategic planning purposes. The interview targets should exhibit a bias toward:

- Clients that represent substantial revenues for the firm;
- Clients that work with multiple partners and/or multiple areas of practice at the firm;
- Clients who give a substantial share of their legal work to the firm – but not all of their legal work (i.e. clients who can compare the firm to others); and
- Clients with multiple years of experience working with the firm – perhaps even who have a multi-generational relationship with the firm.

Ideally, interviews should be conducted by someone other than the partner(s) who typically manage the client relationship. Further, in an ideal setting all of the interviews should be conducted by one or relatively few people (e.g. the chief marketing officer, the director of business development, the director of client value, the managing partner, or a trusted outside consultant).

Ideally, interviews should be completed in a defined two- to three-week window – allowing for the convenience and scheduling needs of the clients. A defined window provides a snapshot of client perspectives at the point in time when the firm is preparing for strategic planning. Obviously, if client feedback is gathered on a continuous basis (e.g. two or three interviews per month), that input is valuable and entirely valid for planning purposes. The "snapshot in time" approach simply reflects an ideal approach when other feedback is not readily available.

While questions can and should be tailored to the firm and its relationship with clients, three broad topics are generally useful for strategic planning purposes:

- First, some reflection on past performance is useful and clients expect to discuss their direct experiences working with the firm and its people (i.e. what the firm has done well historically and how and where it can improve);
- Second, some level of comparison to expectations and (ideally) to competitors is valuable – this should include a discussion of how the firm performs relative to clients' expectations of value (e.g. quality and results relative to the fees charged); and
- Third, clients can be extremely helpful in looking to the future – relative to their own business (e.g. the trends they see and the business challenges they anticipate for the future), relative to their legal and/or business advisory needs, and relative to their direct relationship with the firm (e.g. their advice to the firm in the context of strategic planning).

A generic set of questions – drawn from a variety of past interview guides – should form some combination of the following.

- In providing these services to you, what does our firm do well and not so well? In your opinion, what are our core strengths and where can the firm improve its performance?
- What factors (if any) truly set our firm and its attorneys apart from similar law firms? What is unique about our lawyers/the lawyers you work with?
- What (if any) other law firms provide services to you/your company? How would you compare their services and the relationship they have with you to the relationship you have developed with our firm?
- How does our firm compare on an overall value basis?
- What are the key future legal and management trends that you see in your industry and business? What can/should we do to help you address those issues?

- Related to these trends, what do you see that will increase, decrease, or adjust the services provided to your company/organization by outside law firms?
- If you were consulting to our firm on our future direction and had to make a recommendation or recommendations for the firm's future, what would they be? Would you have any suggested strategies for their strategic plan?

Client feedback should be analyzed with an eye toward the themes and responses that recur across multiple interviews. While there will almost certainly be outliers among the feedback received, there will also be strong patterns in the responses. It is those consistent patterns that should inform the strategic planning process. Naturally, any specific opportunities or relationship issues that arise should be flagged for follow-up. Ultimately, this feedback and input should help to validate (or invalidate) internal perceptions of firm strengths and weaknesses.

Peer group and peer firm comparisons

At the risk of encouraging attorneys' natural tendency to rely on precedent to guide decision making and future direction, it is useful to learn from the successes and mistakes of peers. This is particularly true where a particular firm or group of firms have attained outcomes (e.g. market position, financial results, recruiting successes, etc.) that are enviable on some level. Three types of peer group analyses can be helpful for informing the strategy development process.

First, basic statistical analyses can be useful in pinpointing areas of under and over performance on the part of the firm. Published data is a worthwhile starting point for larger firms (e.g. *Legal Week*'s Top 50 data, *American Lawyer*'s AmLaw 200 data, *The National Law Journal*'s NLJ 350 data). However, proprietary sources are also available to most firms.

- Firms using Thomson Reuters' Elite accounting platform now (generally) have access to customized peer comparisons via Peer Monitor.
- Consulting and accounting firms also maintain proprietary peer surveys that provide useful benchmarking information that can inform the strategy process.

Second, attorney and practice rating and ranking companies (e.g. Best Lawyers, Chambers, BRW rankings, BTI rankings, etc.) can provide helpful data to assess peer group and competing firms' (and practices') relative strengths and weaknesses. These rankings, while not entirely clean and objective, do provide a solid sense for which competitors are perceived as having the strongest lawyers and the strongest practices across most specialties and many sub-specialties as well.

Third, it is often valuable to target one or a few firms for more in-depth study as case models – either in a specific area where they have been particularly successful or more broadly because of the progress they have achieved as a firm (e.g. growth, profitability, reputational, etc.).

Because firms have inherent incentives to publicize their strengths and successes – both on their own website and via public relations efforts – there is ample source material to build informative cases. In addition, the legal press is reasonably adept at researching and publishing cautionary case studies (i.e. in-depth stories covering the decline and/or demise of once successful firms).

Other external trends and business drivers

Chapter 6 in this book provides high level background on a number of the major trends influencing the future of the legal industry. Each firm is unique and legal industry "mega-trends" wax and wane in their relative importance and influence. With that caveat in mind, building a shared understanding (via research and background reading) of external trends is an important aspect of preparing for strategic planning.

Background reading should extend beyond legal industry trends. For instance, developments in the law – particularly in areas critical to core practices in the firm – lend themselves to inclusion in the development of background information for the strategy process. Likewise, industry developments that will have a substantial impact on major clients and/or practice areas should be included in background development.

Strategic issues

The background analyses discussed above can generate a substantial volume of material. That volume of material needs to be made digestible by those charged with drafting and developing the strategic plan. The best means for turning this volume of material into a useful digest of foundational analysis is to knit the internal and external analyses together into a classic SWOT assessment (i.e. Strengths, Weaknesses, Opportunities and Threats).

- For instance, partners' perceptions of firm strengths and weaknesses can be informed and expanded upon via integration of client input, financial analyses and other data; and
- External opportunities and threats begin from clients' perceptions, but are deepened and strengthened by competitive assessments and the facts associated with "mega-trend" background data.

In addition to the SWOT assessment, the initial vision expressed by partners and others should be summarized as part of the foundational digest. That initial vision can be further illuminated by highlighting strategic options available in the external market (i.e. drawn out of the external research) that can enable the firm to achieve that vision

Finally, the entire planning process benefits from having all of the background material reframed as a series of strategic issues. Well-framed strategic issues include two elements:

- A summary heading or phrase that provides a name or label for the issue; and
- A set of strategic questions that need to be addressed and resolved in the context of the strategic plan.

Taken together, the headings and the questions provide a checklist for the planning process. They provide an easy and relatively short point of reference for the large volume of background information developed via the analyses discussed above. For the overwhelming majority of firms, the list of strategic issues can be condensed to eight to 12 headings. The questions draw a well-informed professional back to the implications uncovered via the much more extensive background analyses.

References

1. Legal Marketing Association: www.legalmarketing.org/
2. National Association for Law Placement: www.nalp.org/
3. The Vault: www.vault.com/company-rankings/law/vault-law-100
4. Chambers Associate: www.chambers-associate.com/home

Chapter 3: Phase II – Setting strategic direction

The second phase of the strategic planning process focuses on the long-term horizon for the firm or practice group. Specifically, setting strategic direction involves defining where (directionally) the firm is going over the long run. Similar to Alice's amusing conversation with the Cheshire Cat, if you do not have a particular destination in mind, "it doesn't matter which way you go".

A well-articulated strategic direction generally involves some combination of vision, mission, and primary goals. This chapter will discuss each component in some depth. Following the discussion of the components of strategic direction, steps for developing (and achieving consensus on) a strategic direction will be presented.

Vision

Vision and mission are often used interchangeably in conversation. While definitions vary, vision is generally focused squarely on the future. Mission statements include considerations of the past, present, and future (more on mission in the next section).

The business dictionary defines a vision statement as:

> *"An aspirational description of what an organization would like to achieve or accomplish in the mid-term or long-term future. It is intended to serve as a clear guide for choosing current and future courses of action."*

This is a solid definition and the following points should help refine and illuminate that definition for application in a law firm setting.

A vision statement should be brief – ideally, contained in a single sentence (not always possible and never easy). Brevity is helpful, but not at the expense of being understandable. In the best cases, those two – brevity and clarity – accompany one another. A short, easily understood vision can (and should) be communicated throughout the firm.

The best vision statements are inspirational. This perhaps is the biggest challenge in a law firm setting. People are well educated and articulate. They are trained to be critical thinkers and a degree of cynicism is inevitable among a group of lawyers. Yet, the best visions capture people's imaginations and that spark of imagination can be powerful.

In addition, a good vision is verifiable. It sets a substantive target for the long run. In other words, you know when you have achieved it (or what achieving it will look and feel like).

A few examples of brief, understandable and verifiable vision statements can help to illustrate the point more clearly.

NASA vision example

In May 1961, John F. Kennedy, during a special address to a joint session of the US Congress, offered the following vision for NASA and its Apollo program:

> *"Land a man on the moon and return him safely to earth by the end of the decade."*

That vision is remarkably short. While it was entirely unclear at the time how that vision would or could be achieved, it was easily understood – both by the scientists, engineers, and astronauts directly challenged by the vision, as well as by the nation and the world. Finally, that vision was clearly verifiable – either you reached the moon and returned safely to earth, or you did not.

That statement of vision had a relatively long horizon by business standards – a nearly 10-year "deadline". However, it was enormously ambitious in the early years of the space race. Further, it was inspiring to an entire generation of people at NASA. When Armstrong, Aldrin, and Collins returned to earth in July 1969, that vision had been fulfilled and the organization (and nation) took tremendous pride in the achievement.

McCaw communications example

McCaw Communications was an outgrowth of a cable television conglomerate. The cable company had grown throughout the 1970s via acquisition. The company's CEO, Craig McCaw took a direct and keen interest in cellular communications when the Federal Communications Commission (FCC) held a lottery to award cellular licenses in the early 1980s. McCaw won a few of those licenses and acquired a number of others from lottery winners disinterested in starting and operating cellular networks.

McCaw Communications adopted a succinct vision statement for its new cellular division in the early 1980s:

"Connecting people to people, not to places."

This vision recognized the unique nature of cellular communications long before mobile phones became second nature to us. Clearly the statement is short – and it made cellular communications understandable for the average employee at McCaw. On one level it is verifiable (i.e. if the network works and people are connecting through their cellular devices, the vision has been achieved).

The company grew aggressively throughout the 1980s and early 1990s via acquisition – including acquisition of MCI's cellular division in 1986. McCaw sold its cable division – it was incompatible with the vision. Ultimately, McCaw Communications was sold to AT&T Wireless in 1994 for over $11 billion. By then, the vision was clearly achieved. While the vision never included a financial component (and the McCaw brothers took significant financial risks in pursuit of the vision), achievement of that vision had a substantial financial payout in the end.

Ford Motor Company example

After a couple of false starts in the automobile manufacturing business, Henry Ford and the Ford Motor Company found real success with the Model T – a car introduced in 1908 at a price of $825 (roughly $22,500 in today's dollars). At the time, the Model T was by far the most affordable car in America and it led Ford to adopt a simple vision:

"Produce a car everyone can afford."

This vision is remarkably short (only six words) and is easily understood. Achieving it required some substantial innovations. For instance in 1913 Ford introduced assembly line production (with help from a number of creative employees) driving productivity up significantly. By 1914, the price of a Model T had dropped to $360 and volumes grew to nearly a half million vehicles per year.

Ford also introduced a high-pay workforce concept in 1914 – more than doubling the prevailing daily wage by creating the "Five dollar workday". The increased pay enabled all of Ford's workers to afford Model T automobiles. It also dramatically reduced employee turnover and attracted the best mechanics in Detroit to Ford.

By the mid-1920s, over 15 million Model Ts had been sold. Most people in the 20s learned to drive in a Model T. The vision was verified in the experience not only of Ford's workforce, but ultimately of the American experience in the early 20th century.

A final note on vision

Before turning to the broader concept of mission statements, one other point worth noting is the context of strategic planning. Namely, stating and drawing people to a compelling vision has its origin in spiritual movements. Some of the most influential visionaries in history were essentially religious and spiritual leaders – Abraham, Moses, Jesus, Mohammed, Gautama Buddha, among others, have literally moved billions with their visions over millennia.

In contrast, as will be discussed in a subsequent section, strategy has its origins in the military. It underscores the Japanese proverb – "Vision without action is a daydream. Action without vision is a nightmare."

Mission

Mission statements generally include the vision (note: some firms prefer to keep the vision distinct and parallel it with the other elements of mission). Mission is a broader concept than vision, encompassing past, present, and future (assuming the vision is part of the mission statement). In addition to the vision, a strong mission statement includes a concise articulation of the firm's core values and its purpose(s).

Collins and Porras, in their well-received and widely read book, *Built to Last*, noted that organizational vision necessarily changes as the external market and the wider world change. However, core values endure over generations. Likewise, an organization's raison d'etre – its relationship to its primary stakeholders – tends to remain stable over time. Collins and Porras called this combination of core values and organizational purpose "core ideology".

Interestingly, the most consistent finding in Collins' and Porras' research on visionary companies involves the importance of "core ideology". Essentially they found that organizations with a strong and enduring "core ideology" (i.e. clear and lasting values and purposes) outperform their competitors. Further, they found three factors drive this performance:

1) The "ideology" is captured and documented formally (i.e. it is written down in an articulate fashion);

2) It is widely communicated and understood within the organization; and
3) Actions flow from the "ideology" (i.e. it is more than words on paper).

Mission combines vision with core values and organizational purpose. It combines the two most powerful and proven elements of long term strategic direction into a single statement. Vision was discussed at some length in the previous section. Values and purposes are explained in more depth here.

Values

Core values represent the enduring embodiment of the culture of the organization. They are the guideposts for behavior and they strongly influence the development of people within the firm.

There is no pre-defined set of correct organizational values in a law firm setting. Certainly no firm would embrace poor quality or loose ethical standards (i.e. there are some obvious values that do not work). However, there is a wide range of values that do work for different firms and that help to define different cultures. So, for instance, you will see two firms in the same market – one embracing "hard work" and "entrepreneurism" and the other embracing "strong relationships" and "teamwork." Both can be highly successful, but the culture and tone of each firm will be quite different.

Values provide a form of control within the firm. This is not control in the accounting sense (i.e. creating secure, documented paper trail for cash), but rather in a cultural sense. Organizations with strong cultures and enduring values develop people who are comfortable operating within the boundaries that those values create. People who enter the organization laterally adapt to the culture or end up uncomfortable (sometimes even leaving due to the lack of cultural fit).

Thus, when firms talk about the importance of finding a solid cultural fit when considering mergers or other combinations (or major lateral hires), it is not simply "public relations speak". On the contrary, combining dramatically different cultures is extraordinarily difficult – perhaps more difficult than combining two firms with different economics (e.g. rates, profitability, etc.).

Firms within a particular legal market will often be known within the legal community primarily by their cultural traits – even if that culture is described somewhat derogatorily by their competitors (e.g. "the lifestyle firm," "the sweatshop"). Other factors (including who the leading clients are, who the firm's leading partners are, diversity of the partnership and the workforce, etc.) will be a secondary means for describing them to newcomers or to legal recruits.

Purposes

Purposes respond to the needs of a firm's primary stakeholders. For most law firms (and practice groups), the primary stakeholders are clients, employees, and partners. Some may parse employees into attorney, paraprofessional, and support staff categories, which is fine (and to some extent reflects the culture and values of the firm).

Beyond their primary stakeholders, law firms serve a broader array of stakeholders as well. For instance, the community at large, the local/state/national bar and/or the profession, vendors, and others are clearly stakeholders. However, it is the primary stakeholders that help to define the central purpose(s) of the law firm.

Articulating purposes in a law firm environment is generally a function of understanding what primary stakeholders need the firm to do for them in a superior manner. It is an articulation of why the firm exists – above and beyond making a profit – viewed from the perspective of the stakeholders most directly depending on the firm to do well by them.

This last point – above and beyond making a profit – is important. Recall the Drucker quote in the executive summary of this report.

> *"A company's primary responsibility is to serve its customers. Profit is not the primary goal, but rather an essential condition for the company's continued existence. There is only one valid definition of business purpose: to create a customer."*

Profit is necessary to sustaining the firm into the future. However, if that is the only purpose of the firm, it almost certainly will not last beyond a single generation – mainly because other primary stakeholders (i.e. that do not own the firm and share its profits) will not be well served over the long run. Profit is necessary (vital), but not sufficient.

Mission – public or private document?

The question often arises when a law firm begins to develop or edit its mission statement, "Is this a public document for external audiences or a private document for internal audiences?" The short answer is that mission statements are intended for an internal audience and should be developed with that as the objective.

The longer addendum to that answer is that, once completed, a firm almost certainly won't be ashamed of anything in its mission statement and will have no qualms about sharing it with clients or other external audiences. However, if a firm begins the mission development process with the objective of creating a statement for the website or for marketing purposes, it almost certainly will water down some aspect of the mission to ensure it "sounds good to clients". Mission statements are not marketing devices – they are an articulation of the vision, values, and purposes of the firm.

Dissecting an example

Sidley has put its mission statement on its website, providing an opportunity to dissect one example in the public domain. This is not intended to be an endorsement of the firm or its mission, but simply provides a means to illustrate how a firm combines vision, values, and purposes in a single, concise mission statement.

For those unfamiliar with Sidley, it is one of the largest and most profitable firms in the world. The firm has over 2,000 attorneys in the US, Europe, and Asia. It has one of the most recognized and respected "brand names" in the US.

Sidley's published mission statement is:

The mission of the firm is:

- *to provide the highest quality of professional service to our clients;*
- *to adhere to the highest ethical standards;*
- *to offer our skills and talents for the betterment of the legal profession and the diverse communities in which we practice;*
- *to maintain a culture of collegiality in which we help each other to best serve our clients, our profession and our communities; and*
- *to develop, support and encourage new generations of lawyers to carry on our commitment to excellence, integrity, diversity and collegiality.*

Interestingly, Sidley does not express its vision in this statement. Given the highly competitive nature of the global legal industry, Sidley may have intentionally kept its vision private rather than "tip its hand" to competitors vis-à-vis its aspirations. Or, this statement may have intentionally focused on values and purposes.

The statement does provide an exceptional example of how a law firm talks about its values and its commitments to key stakeholders:

- It promises "highest quality… professional service" to clients;
- It commits its "skills and talents to the betterment of the legal profession" and local communities; and
- It promises to "develop, support and encourage" its more junior professionals.

The statement also highlights a number of values:

- Upholding ethical standards;
- Excellence, integrity, diversity, and collegiality; and
- A culture of collegiality in which we help each other.

On balance, this relatively short mission statement makes its commitment to key stakeholders (people, clients, communities, the profession) and its culture expectations clear and compelling. It isn't a catchy marketing tagline, but there is certainly no reason to keep it a secret – clients and prospective employees are likely to be attracted by the ideas captured here.

Primary excellence goals

The final element of strategic direction is primary excellence goals (PEGs or primary goals for a shorthand term). Primary excellence goals are the focal point for resources – directing time, money, and other resources toward a limited number of areas. The key is to focus on a few areas that can have a real impact on competitive positioning and results. Primary excellence goals define the basis on which the firm (or practice group) intends to distinguish itself and on what basis it intends to compete in the external marketplace.

Note that it is not enough to attain excellence and superiority in any area. Rather, the firm needs to focus on attaining excellence in areas that will help to determine the outcome of competition in the legal marketplace. That competition is largely concentrated in two areas – competition for clients and competition to attract and retain the best people.

In a law firm setting, primary excellence goals will generally involve some mix of two considerations. First, one or more goals will genuinely focus on differentiating the firm (or practice) from other competitors – in the eyes of clients, professionals, or ideally both. Given the fragmentation of the legal marketplace, differentiation is not easy (i.e. general practice firms can look very similar to one another from the outside). The value of achieving a differentiating goal is that it will often be extraordinarily difficult for a competitor to imitate or copy that advantage going forward.

Second, one (or likely several) goals will focus on achieving excellence in areas that are thresholds for competitive credibility. In essence, this second area of focus represents a form of competitive "table stakes". If your firm cannot achieve a degree of competitive excellence in these areas, the firm will be eliminated from serious consideration by professionals and/or clients.

As an example of the former – a differentiating goal – consider how effectively a few New York law firms have positioned themselves as "the safe choice" in the board room for significant financial transactions. For instance, Skadden Arps positioned itself as the most aggressive and knowledgeable firm in mergers and acquisitions – beginning from Joe Flom's focus on shareholder derivative actions, growing in the era of corporate takeovers, and eventually becoming one of the largest and most profitable firms in the world.

As an example of the latter – a "table stakes" or credibility goal – consider the importance of recruiting, developing, and retaining talent (even in the environment of constrained demand growth that the industry has seen since the recovery from the great recession). It is difficult for any firm to truly differentiate itself on the basis of its recruiting or professional development programs. However, no firm can afford to fall behind competitively vis-à-vis people development and retention.

A few critical observations and lessons regarding primary excellence goals are in order.

Observation	Lesson
Consistent, focused application of superior resources is necessary to develop and maintain PEGs	Only a limited number of PEGs can be developed (for most firms, four or five PEGs is a maximum)
Strong PEGs rely upon widespread inter-practice and inter-office cooperation	PEGs must be consistent, mutually reinforcing, and aligned with culture
Developing sustainable PEGs takes time and resources	Whenever possible, PEGs should be built on existing strengths

Displacing a mature competitor from an established PEG is always expensive and often impossible	Seek PEGs that exploit emerging trends and capture unoccupied market positions (so-called "Blue Oceans")
The value of PEGs changes over time	Constant monitoring and evolution of PEGs is required to achieve sustained strategic success

There is a shorthand set of criteria that can help to winnow potential primary excellence goals. Envision the firm having achieved the goal and ask three questions.

1) Is our leadership position in this area providing us with a competitive advantage?
2) Is the achievement of this goal enabling us to satisfy a major stakeholder or stakeholders?
3) Is our achievement of this goal contributing to positive financial results?

If you can answer yes to at least two of these questions, the goal might be a good candidate for focus and development.

A final note on primary excellence goals

It was noted earlier that vision has its origins in spiritual movements, while strategy has its origins in military thinking. Thus, vision and mission are the "spiritual side" of the strategic direction. Primary excellence goals represent a transition toward the military (actually, the competitive) side of the strategic direction.

Developing strong, sustaining, primary excellence goals requires the application of strategic thinking (discussed in more depth in the next chapter of this book). At the most basic level, strategic thinking is:

- **Long-term** (a good planning horizon for law firm PEGs is three years);
- **Relative** in the sense that the firm does not exist in a vacuum, but rather operates in a competitive environment; and
- **Lateral** – strategic thinking cuts across the firm and reflects an understanding of how things relate to one another (as noted in the table above – strong PEGs rely on inter-practice and inter-office cooperation).

Process design – developing strategic direction

The discussion above provides definitions and examples of the central elements of strategic direction – vision, mission, and primary excellence goals. This section provides a set of useful tools and techniques for the strategic direction phase of the planning process. These tools and techniques build on the analytical phase described earlier.

Scenario-based vision development

Scenario-based planning will be discussed in more depth in chapter 7, which outlines strategic planning tools and principles. The following points provide an overview of how the technique can be applied at the vision development and strategic direction setting phase of the strategic planning process.

Scenario planning builds directly upon the extensive external analysis outlined in chapter 2, covering Phase I – Situation analysis. If the firm intends to use scenarios as a tool for vision development, that background work should include research into the major trends influencing the external marketplace. That would likely include trends in the competitive legal marketplace (e.g. consolidation and mergers, the growing focus on alternative fee arrangements, the rising influence of legal operations professionals in corporate legal departments, trends related to entry level salaries, etc.), trends influencing key industries served by the firm, trends in key areas of law, demographic trends, etc.

These trends and other research can be used to highlight major drivers of the future competitive environment (so-called scenario drivers). It is helpful to both define the scenario drivers and to organize the background analyses by scenario driver. That will help the planning team to develop a familiarity and comfort with the scenario drivers and their implications for the firm.

The research will point to a range of possible directions or trajectories those scenario drivers can take over the next five to ten years. Scenario based planning will rely on projections and descriptions for that range of potential future outcomes vis-à-vis the drivers. It should also highlight interdependencies among the scenario drivers. Further, it should highlight the most likely or most probable outcomes.

Using a combination of logic and creativity, two or three future scenarios can be described based on the range of potential outcomes the drivers may exhibit – and the logical interdependencies among the drivers. Those future scenarios should provide a narrative description of an alternative future state – with some clear linkages to how the scenario drivers are influencing that future. It is often helpful to provide a colorful name for each scenario.

The planning team can then use the future scenarios to craft a vision for the firm (note: the scenarios can also inform the selection of primary excellence goals). The team should focus on creating a vision that – if achieved – would position the firm well regardless of which scenario is in play.

The idea is not to predict the future. Rather, the idea is to develop a genuine understanding of what the future may hold – and what factors will most strongly influence the future. The team can then use that depth of understanding of what the future might hold to craft a vision (and/or set of primary goals) that will be good for the firm regardless of what the future actually holds.

Going-in vision exercise

A useful exercise at the start of a vision development or strategic direction setting workshop or meeting is called "going-in vision". This exercise is best done before any real discussion of vision, mission, or goals is undertaken – essentially at the top of the meeting agenda.

The exercise involves having each member of the planning team quietly write down their thoughts completing the phrase, "I would be proud of our firm in five years if..." Once individuals have jotted down their thoughts, ideas should be captured on flip charts – either by going around the table or through an open discussion.

As an added element, follow the "I would be proud" discussion with a second round of quiet thought. The follow-up phrase to be completed: "My greatest fear for our firm over the next five years is..." This darker side of the future can be helpful in generating creative ideas.

The resulting flip chart points can hang in the meeting room throughout the strategic direction setting workshop/meeting. They will spur ideas, confirm later insights, and provide grist for the difficult task of drafting the actual vision and mission statements.

Headlines exercise

Another useful exercise for vision development involves thinking about the firm in the distant future. Depending on the size of the planning team, it may be helpful to form subgroups (break-out groups) of six to eight people to work on this exercise.

The exercise itself asks each group to work on headlines and sub-headlines that describe the firm after it has completed a "ten year run of remarkable success". The publication can be selected to suit the firm (e.g. a local business weekly, the *Wall Street Journal*, the *American Lawyer*, *Legal Week*, the *Financial Times*, etc.).

The exercise has two primary benefits. First, it puts the group ten years into the future – which often helps lawyers to suspend judgment (at least for a little while). Second, it forces the group to boil their thoughts down to a major headline and perhaps a half dozen sub-headlines, driving toward the brevity needed later when it becomes time to draft the vision and mission.

Stakeholder needs assessment

The stakeholder needs assessment is a simple and direct exercise, useful in illuminating core purposes. It builds on the knowledge gained via client input, internal surveys of attorneys, and other background analyses.

Each major stakeholder is discussed in turn. The group is simply asked to identify what the firm (or practice) needs to fulfill in a superior manner to satisfy each stakeholder group. The planning team may want to parse the stakeholders as part of this exercise – which is fine if time permits, but in the end usually does not add tremendous insight

Capture the key points made and agreed upon relative to stakeholder needs. They will be useful when the group begins to draft (or refine the existing) mission statement.

Values trade-offs

Ideally, the group should have input via the internal survey and/or internal interviews regarding core values. As noted in chapter two, either closed-ended and/or open ended questions should have explored organizational values. That is extremely useful for isolating the core values of the firm.

In addition, there are occasions when cultural change is needed. That change may be subtle or it may be dramatic. One tool that can help isolate areas where values (or prevailing strategies) need to change is the values trade-offs exercise.

Members of the planning team are presented with a list of values trade-offs (none have a pejorative ring – thus, the trade-offs will not include "high integrity vs low integrity" for instance). Each member of the planning team rates each trade-off twice. First, they rate the trade-off relative to how the firm currently strikes a balance along the scale. Second, they rate each trade-off relative to how the firm should strike that balance in the future.

The exercise should focus on no more than ten (and ideally fewer) potential trade-offs. A longer list of potential trade-offs is below:

- Disciplined procedures – Lack of disciplined procedures;
- Being correct – Making progress;
- Cost cutting – Resource allocation;
- Intellectual – Practical;
- Centralization – Decentralization;
- Rational decision making – Gut feel;
- Market leader – Market follower;
- Long-term focus – Short-term focus;
- Group pride – Individual pride;
- Risk taking – Risk averse;
- Look for the next fire – Look at the last fire; and
- Structure – Ambiguity.

Primary excellence goal drafting

Primary excellence goal drafting generally follows earlier discussions of vision and mission. More often than not, a solid draft of the vision and mission has been developed by the time the planning team turns its attention to drafting primary excellence goals.

The most successful approach to drafting primary excellence goals generally involves multiple steps. First, the team simply brainstorms potential primary goals. This should involve true brainstorming (i.e. suspend judgment and capture all ideas regardless of quality or technical fit with the definition of PEGs). Capture those ideas on flip charts and hang them together.

Second, review the ideas filling the flip charts, looking for common themes. Colored markers can help to group the common ideas (e.g. circle "people" related ideas in red, "marketing" ideas in blue, "practice management" ideas in green, and so on).

Third, transfer the strongest themes to a consolidated shortlist (i.e. a fresh flip chart). The group can then work to draft primary excellence goals from this shortlist. At this point the group can apply the criteria questions to the shortlisted ideas (e.g. source of competitive advantage, satisfies stakeholder(s), positive financial impact).

A helpful approach to drafting primary goals is to create a short label or title for each goal. A more descriptive expression of the goal can then follow. A few quick examples:

- **Outstanding people and culture** – professionals and staff engaged and involved in a positive work environment;
- **Thought leadership** – identifying and capturing high end niches that distinguish the firm; and
- **Superior, practical results** – timely and efficient delivery of creative solutions to complex legal and business challenges

Final thoughts on the strategic direction development process

One final set of thoughts on developing strategic direction (or any other element of the strategic plan for that matter). Larger planning teams are great relative to building consensus and getting diversity of thought into the process. However, large groups often get bogged down when it becomes time to draft specific elements of the strategic plan.

Whenever the planning team loses focus and/or momentum, consider breaking into smaller groups to complete the exercise or drafting assignment. The general rule of thumb should be: "When in doubt, break them out." Smaller groups can work more productively under an agreed timeframe. The full group can then reassemble to review the results of the smaller teams.

If there is further need to craft a single work product from the work of the smaller group (for instance to get to a single draft mission statement based on the work of two or three smaller teams), steal a page directly from the drafters of the American Declaration of Independence. The committee formed to draft the declaration assigned drafting duties to the best writer in the group (Thomas Jefferson). Appoint your own Thomas Jefferson to prepare drafts for review, revision, and refinement by the full planning team.

Further reading

For those interested in further reading on the primary excellence goal concept, its originator was Cuno Pumpin, then a Professor of Business Administration at the University of St Gallen in Switzerland. In his book *The Essence of Corporate Strategy* (1987) he described the concept as "Strategic Excellence Positions" or SEPs (essentially to maintain the acronym across English and French translations).

For those interested in the more challenging topic of differentiating PEGs, the best approach to the topic can be found in Hamel and Prahalad's *Harvard Business Review* article, "The Core Competence of the Corporation" (1990). While Hamel and Prahalad's work on core competencies was independent of Pumpin's, it gets to the essence of differentiating PEGs.

Chapter 4: Phase III – Strategy development

Strategy development follows the completion of a draft strategic direction (vision, mission, and primary excellence goals). It principally involves two activities:

1) The development of action oriented strategies that allocate resources to the achievement of one of the firm's primary excellence goals; and
2) The development of high level objectives that measure progress toward the achievement of the PEGs.

Strategy development

Strategy development is a function of answering the question, "What are we going to do to achieve each primary excellence goal?" The process begins with a blank sheet of paper with the primary goal listed at the top – a formidable challenge. That challenge can be met with a deeper understanding of strategic thinking – its military origins and principles, as well as its business and organizational counterparts.

In addition, it is vital to comprehend and accept another substantial challenge related to strategy development. Namely, allocating resources and setting strategies requires making difficult choices about what the firm (or practice) will do and what it will not do with time, money, and other resources. Making those choices and trade-offs may be the most difficult part of strategic planning – certainly more difficult than confronting the blank page intelligently.

Strategic thinking

The origins of strategy are often attributed to Sun Tzu, a Chinese general who is believed to have lived around 500 BCE. Sun Tzu's *Art of War* is a favorite source of quotes and insights on strategy. Likewise many writers point to the ancient Greeks as the originators of strategy – the term strategy is derived from the Greek *Strategos*, meaning army leader.

There are three important principles of strategy drawn from that history that should be understood by the law firm planning team.

The advantage of mass or scale

This principle makes the simple point that, all other things being equal, the bigger force wins. This principle has been put to use by a number of law firms and practice groups over the years. The lead debtor in possession counsel role in US bankruptcy cases are almost always filled by one of a handful of firms (e.g. Kirkland & Ellis, Weil, Gotshal & Manges, etc.). Large scale litigation flows to larger regional and national law firms. Fortune 500 companies favor large, global law firms. In the post-Great Recession legal industry, we have seen a few firms grow to unprecedented size (see Dentons) and annual revenues top $2 billion at more than one firm (see Kirkland & Ellis and Latham & Watkins).

The superiority of the defense

This principle highlights the point that a superior defensive position can enable a smaller competitor to prevail over a larger force. Reputation and brand may be the most powerful source of superior defense. Wachtel Lipton is the most profitable law firm in the US – despite being considerably smaller than virtually all of its primary competitors. The "invention" of the poison pill defense against hostile takeover and other innovations cemented the firm's reputation.

The strategy of the indirect approach

Recognizing the first two principles (i.e. that scale is hard to overcome and that it is difficult to displace a competitor from a well defensed position), the indirect approach underscores the value of pursuing unoccupied positions. Indirect strategies range from those focusing on niches to those pursuing new and emerging markets. Indirection is the basis for most law firm (and business) strategy in competitive markets. So-called "Blue Ocean" strategy highlights a specific tool that can help firms define and capture these unoccupied market segments.

These principles are instructive and can help a planning team conceive of effective strategies. Generally a firm needs to adopt a combination of strategies across four or five primary excellence goals – some capitalizing on scale advantages, some capitalizing on superior defensive positions, and others pursuing an indirect approach.

It is important to note that these three military principles are inadequate as a foundation for law firm (or business) strategy. Why? Because military principles are focused entirely on defeating an opposing military force. Contrast that to law firm strategy – where the focus is primarily on winning competitively in the pursuit of clients and talented people.

Business strategy needs to add at least four other key considerations to accommodate this need to focus on winning in a competitive marketplace (not on a battle field). These other considerations were touched on briefly in the discussion of primary excellence goals and are expanded upon in the following points.

Relative thinking

Strategy is deployed in a competitive marketplace. Action taken by any competitor can trigger a response from other competitors. Further, a firm's (or a practice's) expertise and other capabilities are evaluated in the context of its competitors'. As a result, law firm strategy needs to drive the firm to a superior position *relative* to its competitors. It also needs to anticipate the reasonable responses those competitors might take to avoid being at a disadvantage. Perhaps the greatest failure to think in relative terms vis-a-vis law firm strategy has been run-up in associate starting salaries (a race that has re-started in recent years). Obviously, whilst many firms could (and did) respond to other firms' salary moves – accruing primarily to the benefit of entry level people – no firm achieved a competitive advantage in recruiting. Corporate clients, meanwhile, are aghast at the thought of paying the rates suggested by those compensation levels.

Lateral thinking

The most powerful strategies draw on multiple strengths simultaneously. They are mutually reinforcing and mutually supportive. They cut across the firm and draw on the deeper wells of expertise (substantive, industry, and otherwise) within the firm. Further, actions within a law firm lead to subsequent ripples within the firm – everything is connected to everything else on some level within the firm. Thus, strategies that take advantage of (rather than fighting against) the interrelated nature of practices and practitioners tend to have a greater positive impact. For instance, law firms with powerful industry oriented practices (e.g. energy, healthcare, etc.) tend to capture significant advantages in the eyes of clients, while simultaneously leveraging the knowledge of people across multiple areas of law more efficiently.

Long range

There is a natural tendency – once primary goals have been agreed upon – to leap to short-term, tactical thinking. If the strategic direction is compelling, people want to start executing against that direction immediately. However, there is real value in thinking about priorities over the longer range (i.e. a one- to three-year horizon) before jumping into near-term tactics. Key choices and trade-offs are best made with that longer horizon in mind – tactics can follow in Phase IV.

Creative thinking

Finally, law firm strategy benefits from a degree of creative thinking. While it is beyond cliché to recommending thinking "outside the box", because lawyers are trained in precedent it is important to break people away from following what other firms are doing. Ultimately, strategy is about being different in ways that lead to a sustainable advantage in the marketplace. That will not emerge without encouraging and embracing creative thinking.

Strategy development – trade-offs and choices

Applying strategic thinking in a law firm setting is primarily an exercise in allocating limited resources in ways that align well with the strategic direction the firm has developed. That strategic direction includes primary excellence goals – some focused on creating differentiated positions and others focused on excelling in areas that are "table stakes" for maintaining a credible competitive position. So, resource allocation is primarily about making choices that create positions of competitive credibility and/or differentiation.

Michael Porter wrote persuasively about the need to make choices and trade-offs to achieve a sustainable competitive advantage in his landmark *Harvard Business Review* article, "What is Strategy?" Essentially, creating a position that is difficult for competitors to imitate requires focusing resources on a unique set of activities. In so doing, resources are not available to do other things. This explains why even the largest global law firms are not truly full service and no one is the leader across all areas of practice.

Michael Treacy and Fred Wiersema's book, *The Discipline of Market Leaders* characterized the fundamental choice to be between a client relationship focus (i.e. customer intimacy), a low cost and efficiency focus (i.e. operational excellence), and an expertise and knowledge-driven focus (i.e. product leadership). In reality, a firm needs to balance these three so-called disciplines. However, there is logic in choosing to emphasize one – particularly for practice level strategy.

Practice portfolio management

Another approach to thinking about trade-offs in the development of law firm strategy involves allocating resources across the firm's portfolio of practices. That includes performing an assessment of each practice's market position (e.g. leader, parity, lagging) based on factors such as the following:

- The **relative quality** of lawyers and/or work produced is a key factor, but is often difficult to rate objectively;
- Practice **profitability** (measured by contribution, realization, revenue per lawyer, net income per partner, or other means) can be an indication of relative market strength. As noted above, profit potential can also serve well as a factor in determining market attractiveness;
- **Market reputation**/perception can be a strong indication of a practice's relative strength. Is the practice considered the leader, among the leaders, at parity with most firms, lagging other firms, etc.? and
- **Market share** – locally, regionally, or nationally – is another key measure of relative market strength. Unfortunately, law firms generally have to rely on the number of lawyers they have in a given area as a surrogate for market share. Nevertheless, share and share growth are good measures of relative market position.

That assessment is juxtaposed against an analysis of the relative attractiveness of each practice's market. Market attractiveness is a function of factors such as:

- **Competitive intensity** – highly competitive markets may not be as attractive as those with less competition;
- **Rate sensitivity** – markets or specialties that do or can bear premium billing are clearly more attractive than those with a high degree of rate sensitivity;
- **Market growth** – an obvious factor in rating the attractiveness of markets;
- **Market size** – a large market is generally more attractive than a small one. A large, growing market is even better; and

- **Settled/unsettled law** – practices in areas with unsettled law (i.e. where risks are higher and thought leadership is highly valued) are more attractive, assuming the practice has the capability to serve clients well.

On a generic level, that portfolio assessment leads to the trade-offs suggested below.

		Market attractiveness		
		High	**Medium**	**Low**
Relative market position	**High**	Invest and grow	Invest and grow	Maintain pursue/ premiums
	Medium	Invest and grow	Maintain	Maintain or divest
	Low	Improve to survive	Improve or divest	Exit

Figure 2: Market attractiveness and relative market position.

Format for strategies

Strategies are best expressed as action oriented statements of intent or direction. A strategy begins with an action verb, followed by a clear statement of how resources will be allocated in support of that action.

As noted earlier, strategies should have a longer term (one to three years) horizon. If a set of strategies appear to be a series of steps, they are almost certainly tactics that can be rolled-up into a broader, longer term strategy. Likewise, if you can envision the strategy being completed within a year, it is probably a tactic.

As a working rule of thumb, fewer strategies are preferred to more. More strategies simply dissipate resources and water down the important trade-offs the firm needs to make in strategy development. So, for a plan with four primary excellence goals, 15-20 strategies should be more than sufficient to put that strategic direction into action. At the end of this chapter, a generic on-page strategic plan provides an example both of the format and the nature of strategies.

Objective development

High level objectives provide a mechanism for measuring progress toward the achievement of primary excellence goals. They can also serve as a high level focal point for implementation management if the firm elects to use balanced scorecard tools to drive implementation (see the next chapter on Phase IV Implementation planning).

Objectives are generally formatted to highlight what is being measured, what the target or benchmark is, and the timeframe for achieving that target. For instance, a financial objective might be formatted as "To achieve five percent growth in revenues per lawyer each year for the next three years".

From a planning process standpoint, it is usually easier for a planning team to develop objectives after the strategies have been developed. That ensures the team not only understands the primary goals, but also the strategies and resource choices that have been made to achieve those goals.

Most planning teams can brainstorm potential measures readily. Further, most planning teams are good at narrowing the list of potential measures to one or two high level measures for each primary goal. However, planning teams are usually not well positioned to set specific targets in a workshop setting. With measures agreed upon, some research into historical performance against those measures is needed to inform the process of setting targets for the future. With that historical data in hand, the planning team can often agree on finalized objectives informally.

A final caveat regarding objectives

Some goals do not lend themselves readily to quantitative measures. For instance, people goals can be difficult to measure quantitatively. Thus, it is often worthwhile to mix one or more milestone oriented objectives into the strategic plan. High level milestones can provide the same type of useful feedback relative to whether the strategy implementation is leading to the achievement of the primary goals.

Chapter 5:
Phase IV – Implementation planning

The final phase of the strategic planning process is implementation planning. For many law firms, the planning team will be anxious to begin talking about and planning for implementation once a compelling strategic direction is in hand (i.e. at the end of Phase II). As noted earlier, Phase III is important in that it forces trade-offs in resource allocation (before implementation tactics are developed and adopted). Phase III also produces high level objectives – which are particularly valuable if the firm intends to use a balanced scorecard approach to managing implementation.

The energy and enthusiasm for implementation planning is good – it will be needed. The process itself is not easy, since it requires a significant degree of discipline to get into the details of tactical planning. In addition, implementation planning should include at least a first pass at prioritization of the implementation initiatives. So, while there is generally energy going into Phase IV, the process will easily consume that energy.

There are two reasonable options relative to implementation planning. One involves developing straightforward action plans and related supports. The second involves taking a balanced scorecard approach to implementation. Each is discussed below.

Action planning approach

Action planning generally puts the focus for implementation activity at the firm level. It is possible to cascade that to the practice groups, particularly if the firm updates practice level plans on a regular basis. Action planning involves three primary considerations: direct action plans (i.e. defining projects and initiatives, assigning responsibility, and identifying timeframes or milestones); prioritization of those action plans; and organizational and indirect support for implementation.

Direct action plan development

Direct action plan development is an uncomplicated process, but requires discipline and hard work. The process involves putting each strategy on the firm's one page strategic plan into an implementation context. So, if the firm's strategic plan includes 20 strategies, action plans will be needed for each.

The following worksheet can help keep the direct action planning process organized (note: in practice it is generally easier to format the worksheets as landscape pages – providing room for narrative description/notes).

Primary exellence goal:			
Strategy:			
Projects/ initiatives	**Responsibility**	**Timing/milestones**	**Notes**

The first two rows are self-explanatory, they simply provide a placeholder to keep track of the goals and strategies being addressed on each action planning worksheet.

The **projects/initiatives** column is used to identify and briefly describe the implementation initiative to be undertaken. The description should be sufficient so that the responsible person or committee knows what they have been charged with leading. Likewise, the description should be descriptive enough so that partners not directly involved in plan development will understand what the project is.

Projects/initiatives should not include detailed project work plans. The responsible person or committee will be expected to work out the details for the project/initiative. Some initiatives will be quite direct – essentially one step policies to be adopted by the responsible person/people on an ongoing basis (e.g. "Eliminate the marketing committee and delegate that duty to representatives of all major practice groups"). However, most initiatives will require multiple steps and the responsible person or people will need to develop more detailed plans behind the implementation planning worksheet.

Responsibilities should, whenever possible, be assigned to individuals rather than committees. Certainly the governance and organizational structure of the firm will dictate responsibilities in many cases. However, selected projects and initiatives provide excellent opportunities to develop new leaders and spread responsibility beyond "usual suspects". So, look for projects that can be delegated to managers and attorneys who can benefit from taking on new responsibilities and the accompanying experience.

Timing and milestones serve two purposes. Because time is so limited in a law firm, the timing column needs to be used as a reflection of priorities (more on prioritization below). In addition, the column provides an opportunity to identify and document important measures (primarily qualitative, but also quantitative) of implementation progress. Those milestones provide a set of micro-level measures to accompany the high level objectives (i.e. the macro-level measures).

Finally, the **notes** column provides a space to capture other information that should be documented in conjunction with the action plans. That might include important budget implications or commitments, inter-relationships or dependencies with other initiatives, and other reference points.

Prioritization of action plans

Priorities are a function of two considerations:

1) The financial impact of the initiative; and
2) The relative strategic importance/impact of the initiative.

Financial impact can span a fairly wide range – from initiatives that have a nearly immediate, positive financial contribution, to initiatives that represent long-term investments. The key is to evaluate all initiatives using the same financial measuring stick.

Strategic importance and impact relies on a more qualitative prioritization scale. Like the financial scale, it is important to apply criteria consistently. Strategic importance criteria can include considerations such as having a positive impact on the achievement of multiple goals; contributing to differentiation; and creating competitive advantages in key respects (e.g. attracting, developing, and retaining people; expanding client relationships across multiple practice areas; achieving recognition as thought leaders in an attractive area of law, etc.).

Juxtaposing those two scales against one another, priorities become clear. Initiatives that are both positive financial contributors and rate highly on strategic importance are clearly high priorities (i.e. home runs). Strategically important initiatives that require long-term investment essentially require the firm to "bite the bullet" and make it a priority. Initiatives that are less important, but have immediate pay back, are secondary priorities – things you should ensure get done in order to pay for the "bite the bullet" initiatives. Everything else can be pushed off if resources are too limited.

Figure 3 provides a visual method for prioritization.

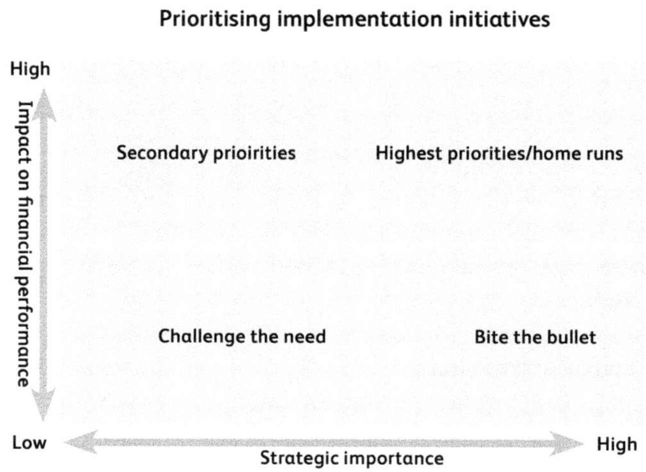

Figure 3: A visual method for prioritization.

Organizational and indirect support

In a perfect world, a firm's strategic plan is built entirely on existing strengths. However, that is not always the case. There may be important practice capability gaps that need to be closed to ensure the effectiveness of an industry-centric strategy. Similarly, there may be important administrative capability gaps (e.g. technology weaknesses, inexperience with legal process outsourcing, etc.).

As a supporting analysis at the implementation planning stage of the process, it can be helpful to assess organizational capabilities in the context of the strategic plan. The emphasis of that assessment obviously should be on ensuring the firm has the capabilities it needs to successfully implement its plan.

An **organizational capability analysis** typically assesses capabilities (where we are and where we need to be) on two dimensions. First, it looks at capabilities relative to competition (i.e. better, worse, or at parity with competition). Second, it looks at capabilities in the context of their respective criticality to the strategy. The resulting analysis creates a matrix on which gaps can be assessed (see figure XX for a sample current state and YY for a sample future state).

This type of gap analysis can lead to a rational set of action plans to close capability gaps and to related metrics and accountabilities to ensure the action plans are carried out. At the end of the process the firm has a solid list of needed capabilities, understandable definitions for those capabilities, and clear action plans and milestones to close the capability gaps. And, done after strategic planning, the capability assessment should be well aligned with the strategy. Note: a balanced scorecard approach obviates the need for this type of standalone assessment.

Finally, **indirect activities** can also strongly support implementation. In fact, indirect steps are often critical to the success of strategic plans. Indirect steps include communications (internal and external communications consistent with and supportive of the plan); symbolic actions such as ceremonies, stories, language and nomenclature, and leadership from the top; and supporting aspects of the firm's culture.

Balanced scorecard approach

A larger scale, but more comprehensive and enduring approach to implementation planning, involves adopting a balanced scorecard approach. My previous publication, *Balanced Scorecards for Law Firms*, details how to apply a balanced scorecard in a law firm environment. The discussion below provides a summary-length discussion of balanced scorecards for law firms.

Balanced scorecard principles

The balanced scorecard was initially developed in the early 1990s in response to the widespread acceptance of shareholder value as the primary (and sometimes only) metric of business performance. It reflected a realization that shareholders' needs had to be balanced with customers' expectations of value. In addition, the balanced scorecard emerged at a time when an alphabet soup of operational management and new technology platforms were competing for management's attention (e.g. TQM, ERP, etc.) as potential "silver bullets" for improved performance. The authors knew that those tools and technologies needed to be directed toward activities that genuinely drove improved shareholder value and/or an improved ability to meet customers' expectations.

At its core, the balanced scorecard is designed to drive strategy implementation – it presumes that an effective vision and strategy already exists. Balanced scorecards connect long-range strategy to the day-to-day implementation of that strategy.

The management approach to do this is deceptively simple. The balanced scorecard involves four fundamental dimensions:

1) **Financial measures** – those measures that define what shareholders (in law firms, the partners) need and expect from the firm financially. In some circles, the balanced scorecard was seen as a backlash against a focus on shareholder value – not true, the system simply recognizes that management needs to balance financial goals with other elements of strategy in order to deliver superior financial results;
2) **Client measures** – those measures that capture how well the organization is meeting client expectations. Simply, how does the organization appear to its clients (e.g. flexible, responsive, intelligent, innovative, providing value, etc.)? Law firms have historically focused on client service and consider that a de facto strength. Yet, many firms do relatively little to measure clients' perceptions of their firm's performance (or even client satisfaction and loyalty);
3) **Learning and growth (human development) measures** – measures that capture how well the firm's people are able to change and improve. Ultimately, is the organization and its workforce getting smarter? In a law firm environment, this involves measuring whether people are more valuable to their clients and colleagues as the market and client needs evolve and change; and
4) **Internal business process measures** – those measures that track improvement in the business processes most important to strategic success. In a law firm environment, that translates to measuring and improving processes that directly impact client experiences and/or financial performance (i.e. tracking improvements that make processes more efficient, more effective, or both).

These four dimensions are not carved in stone – either for companies or law firms. Organizations can and do add new or different dimensions to their scorecards that better fit their business and their primary strategy. However, as a management system, the balanced scorecard as originally designed has proven to be remarkably robust and durable. The evidence has overwhelmingly demonstrated – in industry – that those organizations that use a balanced scorecard clearly out-perform those that do not.

Using the balanced scorecard requires the firm to translate its vision and strategy into meaningful and measurable goals relative to profitability and to client relationships. The strategic plan developed in Phase III will undoubtedly include clear, unambiguous financial targets (e.g. profitability, revenue and/or others). Likewise, the balanced scorecard will require the firm to include a limited set of measurable objectives related to client relationships (e.g. client satisfaction scores, third party rankings/ratings, the number of large relationships the firm has, measures of client diversification, etc.).

Strong firms tend to have mutually reinforcing goals relative to financial performance and client relationships. For instance, over the past 15 years, most general service firms (both mid-size and larger firms) have exited the insurance defense business – why? Because economically, those practices became increasingly incompatible with the shared financial goals of the partners – and the nature of those client relationships became less compatible with the values and culture of full service practices.

With firm level strategy in hand and clear goals articulated relative to profitability and client relationships, the firm needs to engage its practice groups directly in implementation planning. That process will require the practice groups (and their leadership teams) to articulate:

- Their role within the firm and its overall strategy (i.e. how does the practice relate to the firm's overall business strategy, its PPP targets, and its client relationship goals?)
- Action plans (including clear delineation of responsibility/accountability) related to at least three aspects of strategy implementation at the practice group level:
    - What the practice will be doing relative to growing and strengthening client relationships – in ways consistent with the firm level goals?
    - What the practice will be doing relative to the delivery of legal services – both to improve client relationships and to improve financial performance?
    - What the practice will be doing relative to the development of its people (and the tools/technology they will be using) to ensure they are increasingly valuable to clients?

- Practice level measures related to the action plans – in other words, meaningful quantitative and qualitative measures that can be used to monitor progress and hold individuals accountable.

Once the strategy is in place at the firm and practice levels and the balanced scorecards and related action plans are operational, the effort turns to dialog and feedback. The practice groups' balanced scorecards provide the basis for that dialog and feedback. The practices will be pursuing action plans with clear milestones and expectations for particular outcomes relative to financial performance, client relationships, and professional capabilities.

Depending upon the practice group and its role in the firm's strategy, firm leadership should plan to evaluate progress (i.e. have a dialog with practice leadership) two to four times over the course of the year. Those review sessions provide an opportunity for two-way communication – keeping the practices on track and in sync with evolving firm priorities and providing firm management with an early warning system relative to the validity (or invalidity) of its core assumptions and strategy.

On an annual basis, the firm can assess progress against firm level objectives – financial, client relationship, and people related. In addition, firm management can make necessary adjustments in the overall strategy and its guidance to practices. In turn, the practices can incorporate those adjustments into their annual planning – a process that should involve a straightforward updating of the action plans, priorities, and related scorecards.

Chapter 6: Strategic issues – universal challenges to be addressed in the context of law firm strategic planning

There are a number of issues that are virtually universal challenges for law firms – issues that are faced by nearly all competitors in the legal industry. Some have been strategic challenges for decades, others have emerged more recently.

This chapter highlights those universal strategic challenges, and provides some initial framing of the issues for law firm managers. It is by no means a comprehensive review of any of these strategic issues (some have been covered at book length by other authors). Rather, it is a primer that should help law firm leaders prepare for strategic planning.

While these issues are virtually universal across the legal industry, they manifest themselves differently in individual firms. For instance, although all firms confront the same societal demographic trends and issues, the demographics within individual firms can vary substantially. Similarly, while all clients (or nearly all clients) are looking for solid value from their investment in legal fees, some are entirely disinterested in alternative fee arrangements. So, the issues are ubiquitous, but their implications will vary widely from firm to firm.

This chapter will frame and briefly discuss seven strategic issues:

1) Talent management;
2) Client expectations for value;
3) Profit growth and financial management;
4) Succession planning and management;
5) Information management;
6) Disaggregation of legal processes; and
7) Business development and marketing.

Talent management

It has become a cliché, but it is nonetheless true. In a professional service firm, the most important assets of the business walk out the door every night. In that context, talent management issues are in many ways the most pervasive and endemic strategic issues to be addressed in the context of strategic planning.

At core, managing people in a knowledge intensive business such as law requires effective recruiting (entry level and lateral); professional development that enables people to grow and enhance their value to clients; and retention over the long run via tangible and intangible factors (such as compensation, work environment, etc.).

As we approach the 2020s, four interrelated trends will strongly challenge law firm leaders' ability to manage people issues effectively.

Demographics

Most directly and unavoidably, demographic trends will present a significant challenge to law firm leaders over the coming decade. The post-War baby boom (marked by most demographers as 1947-1964) created the largest cohort of people to enter the workforce in history to that point. Further, that large cohort was accompanied by a parallel trend of increasing participation in the workforce by women – thereby increasing the effective size of an already unprecedented cohort.

That boom was followed by a dramatic fall off in the number of births in most western democracies (1965-1980). Thus, after building an infrastructure and an economy prepared to take in large numbers of people (first as students and later as workers), managers had to adjust to an environment with a substantially smaller pool of applicants (Generation X, born 1965-1980). Over the past ten years, Millennials (1981-1996) have begun entering the workforce. Depending on who is measuring (and how they are defined), Millennials are now the largest cohort in history – and this generation is the most racially and ethnically diverse in history.

How is this boom and bust and boom again manifesting itself in law firms and what strategic challenges does that create for law firm leaders?

- The oldest of the Boomer cohort is in their early 70s and we are fast approaching the point at which more than half of all Boomer lawyers are retired. In most firms, some of the most productive people and some of the biggest rainmakers are or were part of this cohort. Effectively managing the remainder of Boomer retirements will be a significant challenge over the coming five-plus years.
- Generation X lawyers are now playing important leadership roles in law firms. Gen X partners are often intensely committed to their

law firms. They are part of a smaller generational cohort, often misunderstood by their Boomer elders. Many were in the formative years of their legal careers during the aughts – seeing both rapid growth, a massive recession (with layoffs at many firms), and flat demand since the recovery. This group had to work hard to succeed in private practice.

- Somewhat ironically, many Gen X law firm leaders complain that Millennial lawyers as a cohort do not share the work ethic of the generations that preceded them. That may or may not be true. What is clear, however, is that associate turnover has returned to rates not seen since the boom years of the mid-aughts. And, even though Millennials are a large cohort (larger than the Boomer cohort), they are not choosing a legal career in the same numbers as Boomers or Gen X.

One final demographic challenge facing law firms is largely unrelated to the boom and bust and boom demographic cohorts. That challenge involves increasing the gender and ethnic diversity of law firms' workforces – and the challenge is particularly acute with regard to increasing diversity in the partnership ranks (roughly eight percent of equity partners in US law firms were minorities in 2018; roughly 15 percent of all attorneys were minorities). Many Fortune 500 corporations now explicitly include diversity metrics in their selection and/or evaluation criteria for outside counsel.

The diversity challenge has two distinct components. Relative to gender diversity, there are (and have been for many years) a substantial number of women graduates from law schools. In fact, women have been in the majority of graduating classes in several of the past ten years. Yet, while roughly 45 percent of all associates are women, only 20 percent of equity partners are women. It would appear that the primary challenge for law firms relative to gender equity is not the number of law school graduates. Rather, the challenge is reconciling firms' career path(s) and work environments with broader societal expectations of young parents.

Relative to ethnic diversity, the challenge begins with the reality that law schools are not graduating diverse classes (certainly not as diverse as the population at large). While women represented nearly half the graduating class of 2018, minorities were roughly 31 percent of the graduating class. That is a marked improvement over the past ten years, but minorities are not going into private practice at the rates of their white counterparts. As a result, there are far too few minorities in private practice to move ethnic diversity numbers at the partner level in the next five or even ten years.

Career paths

The structure of law firms and the legal industry has been evolving, and many predict a continuing evolution in the coming years. It has clearly become more difficult to become an equity partner – particularly in larger firms. The number of non-equity partners has grown, the number of years an associate must work to become eligible for partnership consideration has gotten longer, and Millennials are opting out of law firms at rates not seen since before the recession.

An environment in which fewer people become (or even aspire to become) equity partners represents a significant change in career paths and career planning in law firms. Depending on how the process (and individual career paths) are managed, this can have a substantially positive, substantially negative, or mixed impact on firms. Certainly, those who have historically viewed those not on the equity partner track as so-called "second class citizens" will find it more difficult to retain valuable talent.

Hiring trends

Entry level hiring has returned to levels similar to pre-recession years (i.e. law school graduates are finding work that requires passing the Bar at levels at or above levels experienced in the mid-aughts). Further, law firms represent a growing share of those hiring new law school graduates (46 percent of 2017 US law school graduates were hired by law firms).

Meanwhile, lateral hiring – particularly at the partner level – has increased. The National Association of Law Placement (NALP) reports on lateral hiring every year. Following a sharp decline in the depths of the recession, lateral hiring bounced back significantly in 2011-12. Since then it has increased modestly most years.

Coupled with record numbers of mergers, both partners and associates are changing firms more frequently than at any time in history.

In addition to movement among law firms, lateral movement to other career opportunities has grown over the past several years. In-house departments have grown substantially since the end of the recession. Many alternative legal service providers' (ALSP) business models rest in part on hiring experienced non-partners out of law firms. Those represent attractive career options for law firm associates who do not aspire to partnership.

While all firms are drawing (or can draw) attorneys from the same sources, how and how many people are recruited at the entry level and laterally will have an impact on everything from profitability, to culture, to client satisfaction. Coupled with changing career paths, law firm leaders need to be prepared to manage the hiring process effectively over the coming decade simply to remain effective outside resources for their clients.

Client expectations for value

It has been several generations since attorneys sent their clients one-line invoices reading, "For legal services rendered..." followed by an amount. "Value" has become a buzzword of sorts in the legal industry and it can be defined fairly directly. Value is a direct function of the results delivered in exchange for the fees charged (i.e. Value = Results/Fees).

Understanding four major developments in the legal industry should help law firms respond effectively to clients' expectations for value. The Association of Corporate Counsel's (ACC) "Value Challenge" is a good starting place –it represented a highly publicized demand by in-house counsel and set the tone for what has become a "buyer's market" in the legal industry. The ACC and its value challenge were indirectly responsible for the rise of operations professionals within in-house legal departments. The rise of legal operations (both at ACC and in the emergence of the Corporate Legal Operations Consortium (CLOC)) is a second major development vis-à-vis client expectations. Add to those the rise of alternative fee arrangements (AFAs) – a trend that must be understood in the context of law firm strategy and clients' demands for value. Finally, the move toward disaggregation of the legal process and outsourcing selected elements has an impact on value as well.

The ACC and the "Value Challenge"

The ACC began developing its "Value challenge" in the mid-aughts. In part the idea was motivated by a shared concern among in-house counsel regarding the rapid rise of entry level associate salaries in larger law firms (i.e. firms serving larger institutional clients). The ACC perceived a direct connection between rising salaries and increasing billing rates. Whether there really was a direct connection is debatable – for instance, a strong correlation between PEP growth and rate growth is evident, but the ACC did not appear troubled by growing law firm profitability.

The association's response – several years in the making – was the ACC Value Challenge and a related "Value Index" (ratings by in-house counsel of the value delivered by outside law firms). The index never really gained much traction and has been discontinued. However, the Value Challenge remained a centerpiece and major focal point of the ACC throughout (and even following) the great recession. Importantly, the Value Challenge included some pragmatic approaches to improving value (and client relationships in the process).

The ACC's own description of the Value Challenge and what it covered is:

> *The ACC Value Challenge is an initiative to reconnect the value and the cost of legal services. Believing that solutions must come from dialog and a mutual willingness to change, the ACC Value Challenge is based on the concept that law departments can use management practices that enhance the value of legal service spending; and that law firms can reduce their costs to corporate clients and still maintain strong profitability. The ACC Value Challenge promotes the adoption of management practices that allow all participants to achieve their key objectives.*
>
> *There are many ways to improve value in the firm–client relationship. The ACC Value Challenge focuses on providing resources and training – for law firms as well as law departments – on these key value levers:*
>
> - *Aligning relationships;*
> - *Value-based fee structures - i.e. not based on the "billable hour";*
> - *Staffing and training practices;*
> - *Budgeting;*
> - *Project management;*
> - *Process improvement;*
> - *Use of technology;*
> - *Data management;*
> - *Knowledge management; and*
> - *Change management.*

The Association provided training and a number of related resources. Some focused directly on the "value levers" noted above. Others focused more broadly on a process for improving dialog between in-house legal departments and their outside attorneys. In many respects those resources look remarkably similar to the approach described in an earlier chapter addressing co-creating unique value.

Although the Value Challenge eventually waned, ACC member organizations had begun to invest in operational expertise to drive value and capture some of the promise inherent in the value levers. As a result, the ACC now has a large community of interest among legal operations professionals.

Legal operations

The rise of legal operations within in-house legal departments was a logical outgrowth of both the ACC Value Challenge and other converging trends in corporate legal departments. Many value levers identified in the Value Challenge lent themselves to active management – by professionals focused full time on that function (and not necessarily by someone with a law degree). Corporate finance departments were demanding more predictability and lower overall costs from their legal departments.

CLOC has nearly 1,800 members from over 900 companies in over 40 countries. The organization has grown quickly by focusing on 12 "core competencies" that legal departments need. The competencies are grouped based on CLOC's assessment of what a fully mature legal operation will be capable of managing. To give readers a sense of the ambitious focus of legal operations professionals, below are CLOC's recommended "core competencies".

Foundational competencies include:

1) Financial management – including managing the departmental budget, tracking accruals and forecasting;
2) Vendor management – including creating vendor management programs to insure quality outside counsel support at the right rates and under optimal fee arrangements, as well as governing billing guidelines;
3) Cross-functional alignment – including driving relationships with other key company functions, such as HR, IT, and Finance; and
4) Technology and process support – including creating a long-term technology roadmap.

Advanced competencies include:

5) Service delivery and alternative support models – including utilizing the right resources for the right matters, including using managed services, LPOs, and other service providers and technology as appropriate;
6) Organizational design, support and management – including delivering improved GC Staff and overall team performance within the legal function;

7) Communications – including work collaboratively across the legal ecosystem; and
8) Data analytics – including collecting and analyzing relevant data that drive efficiencies and optimize spend.

Mature competencies include:

9) Litigation support and IP management – including supporting e-discovery, legal hold, document review;
10) Knowledge management – including creating seamless access to legal and department institutional knowledge;
11) Information governance and records management – including managing the records management program; and
12) Strategic planning – including creating long-term strategy and aligning annual goals.

Going forward, firms are going to need to engage with legal operations professionals if they expect to maintain healthy and profitable client relationships.

Alternative Fee Arrangements

One approach in-house counsel has pursued to gain greater predictability and value is alternative fee arrangements. AFAs have been discussed in one form or another for over 20 years (i.e. "We have to get away from the billable hour"). They have grown to become a consistent share of all outside legal work (surveys typically find 20-25 percent of work is being done under some type of AFA).

Some approaches are well known and have been widely discussed – fixed fees for defined matters (e.g. patent prosecution, loan documentation, etc.); contingent fees for litigation and/or collection work; premiums and discounts for transactional outcomes. Others are uniquely developed for a particular client by a particular law firm.

A number of surveys and financial benchmarking companies examine AFAs (e.g. Altman Weil's annual *Law Firms in Transition* survey, Citibank and Peer Monitor tracking of AFAs, etc.).[1] Essentially, the research finds a wide variety of approaches to alternative fees, but those approaches can largely be traced to three underlying motivations (note: the motivations are not mutually exclusive):

1. Some simply need to cut costs. Fee arrangements trend toward discounts and blended rates in these contexts. Many would argue that discounts and blended rates are not AFAs – since they are still largely hourly based charges;
2. Some need predictability, particularly if they have a block of recurring or continuing litigation or transactional work. Fee arrangements in this context trend toward fixed caps for matters – or more often for blocks of business. For continuing relationships built on trust, those fixed fee arrangements can be adjusted annually to bring charges in line with actual ongoing costs (i.e. hours continue to be tracked, but are not the basis for billing); and
3. Some are driven by risk management models or strategies. In this context, fee arrangements trend toward some form of contingency. Contingency arrangements for defense lawyers usually involve agreeing on an overall value (or exposure) for a case, an assessment of positive outcomes and negative outcomes. Work is billed at a discount or there is a holdback – with an upside reward (e.g. closer to standard rates) for an outcome close to an expected outcome and a premium for outcomes closer to the most positive potential outcome. Contingency work for transactional lawyers tends to focus on the value of the deal – with deep discounts for deals not closed and premiums that relate to the size of a closed transaction (a lawyer's version of the Lehman formula).

Understanding a client's motivation(s) for seeking an AFA is critical to narrowing the range of arrangements a firm might suggest. Further, it is imperative that private practitioners understand their own costs and the underlying economics of their practice and their firm. Whether the focus is on managing margins (a fairly high-level instrument) or on managing selected profit drivers, good alternatives cannot be constructed unless the firm understands its own practice economics.

Disaggregating the legal process

Legal Process Outsourcing (LPO) and ALSPs are discussed at greater length in the Disaggregation of legal processes section below. However, in the context of client expectations for value, it is important to recognize that clients increasingly see the logic behind disassembling the legal process so that elements of that process can be done by lower cost resources.

In some contexts, clients want to deconstruct the process so they can in-source work to people in their own departments. In other situations, they believe contract attorneys and/or temporary services are an appropriate resource – and want to realize the savings that go with using those resources. Therefore, process disassembly and deconstruction are not entirely about LPO, but that is a potentially logical response once the process has been disaggregated.

This trend will have a bigger impact on larger firms and those taking on larger scale engagements over time. However, even mid-size firms need to be prepared to think about the legal process in terms of discrete elements – some of which might be better and/or more economically done by someone not directly employed by the firm. That in turn can generate greater value for clients without eroding profitability.

Profit growth and financial management

The growth in law firm profitability is an undeniable strategic trend. Average profits per equity partner (PEP) in the AmLaw 100 in 2017 were over $1.7m, up over five percent from 2016. There were nearly 30 firms with profits per equity partner in excess of $2.0m. Profit management is both a defensive and offensive imperative for firms as we approach 2020.

Because profit numbers are so visible – at least among the larger firms (and well into the ranks of mid-sized firms) – profit management has become a factor in people management. Specifically, profit per equity partner reports contribute to the rise in lateral partner movement. High profitability has positioned some firms to effectively "buy" practices via outsized lateral job offers (e.g. guarantees of very high compensation for two or three years). Further, profitability becomes a factor in every firm's ability to retain key people and to recruit talented people at all levels.

Many firms have clearly tightened their criteria for entry to and continued presence in the equity partnership. Thus, part of the growth of PEP has been a function of managing the denominator. This tendency to manage the denominator is likely to continue into the future. For instance, note the people management trend above regarding the rise of two tiers of non-equity partners and other alternative career tracks.

Setting aside management of the denominator, profitability is generally a function of five factors (see Figure 4). One could add the time value of money to the list, but rates are low and many firms are self-financing entities and thus are not strongly driven by interest rates and the time value of money.

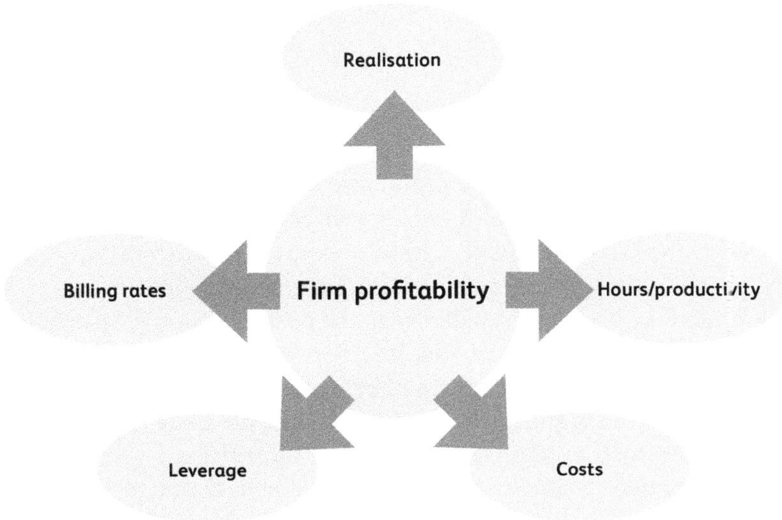

Figure 4: The five factors affecting firm profitability.

Each of the financial levers is discussed in the sections below.

Billing rates

For definitional purposes, billing rates are the standard "published rack rates" for all timekeepers in all client serving departments and/or practice groups (including paralegals, patent agents, engineers and other non-attorney timekeepers). Billing rates are an obvious lever on the revenue side of the profit equation (revenues minus costs).

As noted above, profit growth at many firms prior to the financial crisis was driven by increases in billing rates. In some respects, it was a self-reinforcing cycle. As the largest (and most expensive) firms raised rates, it created a price umbrella under which mid-sized firms could raise rates (and still remain a relative bargain). In the face of so-called "rate compression" the large firms would again be compelled to raise rates and the cycle would repeat itself.

Future profit growth associated with simple rate increases are likely to require more than a letter informing clients of the increase. In fact, those letters are often met with an expectation that the firm will be discounting those rates across the board. Regardless, there will need to be demonstrable value associated with higher rates (i.e. results will need to be superior relative to the rates charged). Or, the higher rates will be realized as a function of alternative fee arrangements (discussed above).

Hours/productivity

Productivity is simply a measure of the number of hours per timekeeper (at the individual and practice group levels). Number of billable hours is a simple and blunt driver of revenues and profitability. Clearly, there are physical limits to the number of billable hours a firm can expect out of a timekeeper – though the range of expectations is quite broad.

Productivity has been a challenge in the post-recession years. Demand for outside legal services (i.e. law firm services) has been relatively flat over the past five years. Meanwhile, firms have been hiring at the entry and lateral levels aggressively. As a result, billable hours per fee earner have not returned to pre-recession levels at most firms.

A key element to understand vis-à-vis billable hours' relationship to firm profitability is that the last few hundred billable hours are generally the most profitable. Essentially, timekeepers work much of the year to cover the direct and indirect costs associated with their employment at the firm. A simple example can help to illustrate the point.

> Imagine for a moment a patent engineer who earns $120,000 annually. In addition, her employment agreement includes employee benefits (retirement funds, insurance, payroll taxes, etc.) that add $40,000 annually in other direct costs.
>
> Further, employing that engineer requires office space and other overheads to provide an appropriate working environment – assume those costs add another $35,000 annually in indirect costs. Thus, total direct and indirect costs for our hypothetical patent engineer are $195,000 annually.
>
> Now, imagine that our engineer's billing rate is $200 per hour. In that simplistic scenario, our engineer is working nearly half the year (1,000 hours – assuming all her time was billable, which of course it is not) simply to cover direct and indirect costs associated with her employment.
>
> If that professional carries a billable hour expectation of 1,500 hours, only the final third of the year actually create profits.

Many tactics are available to incentivize timekeepers to increase their billable hours. That includes published standards (under which it is culturally inappropriate to fall – and may result in symbolic or actual sanctions), billable hour bonuses (for hours above standards), awards and recognition, and other tactics.

Leverage

Leverage in a law firm is defined as the ratio between hours or dollars billed by equity shareholders/partners and hours or dollars billed by all other fee earners. Many crude statistics measure leverage in terms of full time equivalent (FTE) ratios (e.g. number of equity partners to number of other timekeepers). On an even more simplistic level, some measure leverage as a simple ratio of partners to associates.

In a perfect world, where everything else is held constant, increased leverage leads to increased profitability. The reason is easily understood – people other than partners are creating profitable revenues; the more of them there are creating that profitable revenue, the more profitable the firm is.

Unfortunately, we do not live in a perfect world and all other things are generally not held as constants. As noted above, the last 100 billable hours in a year largely fall to the bottom line, while the first 100 simply cover costs. If a firm does not have enough work to keep non-equity timekeepers fully utilized, increasing leverage will tend to increase costs rather than profits.

More importantly, managing leverage should really be a function of getting the right skills and people working on behalf of clients on any given matter. If a matter calls for partner level knowledge and experience, pushing the work down to associates simply to improve leverage does the client a disservice. Conversely, if a partner hordes work to keep his or her billable hours high, some of that work undoubtedly should have been done at a lower rate by less experienced professionals. Again, managing leverage is really about having the right people on the right matters.

Over the long term, leverage becomes a critical profit driver – since the mix of staffing (in a practice and a firm) can be balanced appropriately against the needs of clients. As law firm models evolve over the coming decade, more strategies will be available to firms to manage leverage.

- A wider variety of non-partner track careers are likely to develop in law firms – enabling firms to leverage more experienced and skilled lawyers in new ways (i.e. beyond leveraging non-equity partners);
- Demographic trends in developed economies will encourage firms to retain senior people beyond traditional retirement ages – providing

another option for capturing leverage from experienced, highly skilled professionals;

- Contract attorney business models will continue to expand, providing alternatives for managing capacity and leverage over the short term; and
- Off-shore service providers (e.g. LPO providers) and ALSPs are likely to continue to grow – providing another option for leverage and capacity management.

Realization

Billable hours and billing rates are simply accounting methods if a firm cannot collect the time billed at the rates agreed upon. Realization is a measure of the difference between the net fees collected and the fees that would have been collected had the total hours recorded been invoiced and collected at standard rates.

Realization can exceed 100 percent in instances where premium rates are billed or where matters billed under fixed fee arrangements take less time than originally budgeted. More often, realization falls short of 100 percent due to agreed-upon rate discounts, write-downs of inefficient or unauthorized time, and/or clients object to paying the full amount invoiced. Since the recession, average realization rates have steadily fallen (from the low-to-mid 90 percent range pre-recession to the mid-80 percent range in 2017).

While improving realization would appear to be a financially driven goal, achieving that goal generally requires either an improved client orientation and/or improved business processes.

Client oriented initiatives that improve realization include alignment of staffing with client needs and expectations (i.e. the right people at the right rates on client matters), development of alternative fee approaches, and other steps that lead clients to demand or expect less discounting.

Business processes can improve realization primarily by improving either the legal work process itself and/or the timeliness and accuracy of the billing process. There are almost always inefficiencies in legal work processes, so streamlining and automation can improve realization. Clients' objections to invoices can often be traced to a lack of timeliness in billing (e.g. billing time incurred months ago – by which time the client has forgotten what the value of that time was).

Costs

Costs are largely self-explanatory. In a law firm environment, the overwhelming majority of costs can be traced directly to people – their salaries, their benefits, their payroll taxes, and the space and other overhead required to ensure they can remain productive.

As entry level associate salaries accelerated between 2001 and 2008 – with little impact on rates of associate retention – people related costs grew substantially. It would appear that the salary wars have returned over the past few years – at least in the US legal market. Associate starting salaries have increased in two of the past three years and bonuses have increased substantially as well.

The coming decade offers law firms a wide range of potential cost management strategies and tactics – alternative career paths, outsourcing, virtual offices and telecommuting, and other approaches to managing capacity, personnel costs, and overheads. It is rare for a firm to "save its way to prosperity," but cost management is not an inconsequential aspect of driving profitability. Ultimately, effective cost management in a law firm implies strong people strategies.

Managing the profit drivers outlined above can certainly help firms respond to the broader trend of profit growth and financial management. Two considerations can further enhance a firm's success in managing profits. First, there is a meaningful distinction between short term profit management and longer term profit management. Second, some factors are purely administrative, while others are strategic.

Short- versus long-term profit management

Asked about the long-term impact of deficit spending, George Maynard Keynes was said to have replied, "In the long run, we're all dead". From a law practice management standpoint, in the long run, we should all be financially healthy and profitable.

In the short run, firms and practice groups are generally faced with a choice of taking whatever work is available at the going rate or creating zero revenue. Taking near-term work is marginally better than having no work at all. However, in the long run, firms have considerably greater control over their own financial destiny.

Over the long run, every one of the profit levers outlined above can be adjusted substantially – particularly the mix of people and skills. Practices that do not bring their professional mix into alignment with clients' expectations can expect to suffer. Meanwhile, each of the major profit levers is best managed via an integrated approach. Each profit lever requires considerations beyond the purely financial to have a sustained, positive impact on financial results.

Integrated action on profit drivers (i.e. a long-term approach to profit growth) is often best implemented at the practice group level. Practice groups – in truth, the leading partners in those groups – actively supervise matters, assign work, manage client relationships, train junior lawyers, and frequently prepare and send invoices. Generally, therefore, actions taken at the practice group level can have the greatest actual positive impact on profitability over the long run. That is where the right mix of costs, rates, realization, leverage and productivity can be created in the service of clients. It is the place where client relationships often begin – thus, providing a long-term opportunity to attract the right mix of clients as well.

Administration versus strategy

As the discussions above should have made clear, much of the profit management process requires good management and good strategic thinking. It requires targeting the right kinds of clients, who will derive real value from the capabilities of the firm. It requires developing and maintaining capabilities that have value in the marketplace.

However, there is an administrative aspect of profit management that is occasionally overlooked – namely, good business administration directly contributes to profitability. If billable time is recorded at or near the moment the work is completed, it will be captured more accurately. Timely and accurately captured billable hours are then ready to be invoiced. Timely invoicing ensures clients get bills while they still remember the value delivered on the matters. It is a virtuous circle. Good business hygiene leads to better client satisfaction. That leads to better collections – which in turn improves profitability.

Succession planning and management

As noted in the demographic trend section above, the aging of the baby boomer demographic cohort has led to a substantial wave of partner retirements over the past ten years, with another nearly ten years of retirements in a steady stream still ahead. That wave of retirements creates its own strategic issue – the need to effectively manage succession of retiring partners' practices.

Succession management is a complex – and potentially emotional – issue in most firms. Highly productive and successful partners contribute on so many levels. Their work on behalf of clients (i.e. their billable time) is obviously valuable – often reflecting high rates and contributing strong revenue streams that are not easy to replace (at least directly). They are often primary client relationship managers and rainmakers – the firm clearly wants to retain those relationships after partners retire. Those partners often possess a knowledge base that is both extensive and difficult to capture and pass-on. Finally, those partners generally have relationships beyond current clients that are likely to wither after they retire – relationships that benefit the firm directly and indirectly (e.g. referral sources, community involvement, charitable boards, etc.).

In many firms, the structure of capital buy-outs, funded and unfunded retirement systems, and other incentives directly address the retention of client relationships and other financial contributions. For instance, many systems directly reward departing partners (or emeritus partners) with a share of the revenues flowing from client relationships they successfully leave behind in their wake.

However, financial incentives are only that – an incentive. Successfully transitioning a client relationship generally involves many years of trust and relationship building between younger partners and key people in the client organization. That transition is clearly a two-way street – one that is as much in the hands of the client as it is the relationship partner's to manage succession in relationships.

Handling the succession of the other factors is even more difficult. A career's worth of experience and knowledge cannot simply be written down or transferred into a codified knowledge management system (no matter how robust that system may be). Likewise, personal and professional relationships that are intermittent and not directly related to the delivery of client service are often impossible to transfer. Certainly, a younger person can step onto a charitable board or into a civic organization. However, the relationships they develop will necessarily be distinct from the relationships created by the retiring partner.

As the demographic realities of the retirement wave have become increasingly apparent, more firms are adopting approaches that enable and/or encourage retiring partners to remain involved in the firm on some level. Some already have formal emeritus or senior partner roles in place to retain key people in constructive roles. Some approach the process informally, yet manage to keep people engaged beyond their "official" retirement. Some cross their fingers and hope for the best (not advisable). Whatever approach is feasible in your firm, it will become increasingly important to have an effective method for managing succession in the coming decade – that includes addressing situations in which aging partners essentially refuse to slow down and/or discuss retirement.

Information management

Information management (as distinct from a firm's IT department) is a critically important issue for all professional service firms. This section briefly highlights and discusses three critical aspects of information management in law firms: knowledge management (KM); data science and artificial intelligence; and legal analytics. The lines between these topics may blur, but each warrant separate discussion.

Knowledge management

Knowledge management (KM) and the related systems, processes, and technologies that support it have become well understood and generally embraced in law firms. Most firms of reasonable size have effective document management systems for instance – and many of those systems provide front end search tools. Likewise, firms have taken old fashioned form files and transformed them into more interactive tools. People who have entered the practice in the past ten years take for granted the availability of searchable brief banks, pleadings banks, and other repositories of past work products.

Further, some firms have applied the same tools to the business development and management sides of the law firm. Thus, past proposals and "boilerplate" for responding to various requests for proposal are readily available. Likewise, the ability to find the right people and the right CVs to put into a proposal are served by KM tools and systems. Some have systems that enable attorneys and practice managers to model alternative approaches to staffing matters – both at the proposal stage and for purposes of ongoing practice management.

That general trend is certainly an element for strategic planning and management. Even at its most basic and generic level, KM is an issue – firms and practices need to be able to efficiently and effectively manage (and access) the considerable experience and knowledge of its people. The larger and more dispersed that knowledge is, the more indispensable structured approaches and tools are vis-à-vis KM.

In addition to that foundational level of KM, however, firms should be thinking about the strategic linkages knowledge management has to other strategic issues within the law firm. As discussed immediately above, succession management includes critical considerations relative to the potential for lost knowledge. Training and professional development are aided greatly by an effective KM function and related tools. Further, client relationships can be strengthened and deepened through effective knowledge management (e.g. tracking creative deal terms and suggesting relevant ideas to clients; sharing and working on documents collaboratively; pursuing co-creation initiatives with clients, etc.).

The KM field and the available tools and technologies continue to expand. Certainly, adopting and deploying knowledge management processes and systems is an important first step – one that many firms have taken. The next level in that process is applying KM principles, tools, and practices to client relationships, professional development, succession management, and other strategic issues facing the law firm.

Data science and artificial intelligence

It may be an uncomfortable thing to admit publicly, but a substantial volume of the work done by lawyers (particularly younger lawyers in larger firms) involves repetitive cognitive tasks. That ranges from reading and reconciling countless contracts as part of merger and acquisition projects to document reviews in large scale commercial litigation. Machines can do much of this repetitive cognitive work with greater accuracy and speed – and do it at a dramatically lower cost.

A number of firms now employ (or contract with) data scientists, who specialize in putting machines to work on those repetitive cognitive tasks. This frees up attorneys to focus on tasks that involve analysis and judgement, but it also vacuums a lot of billable time out of big projects. Teams that deliver better quality, more quickly than competitors, should be rewarded. But, if a firm's or practice's mindset revolves around billing hours, giving major tasks to machines (albeit run by professionals) is not particularly attractive.

Further, given time, the machines can be programmed to learn and recognize patterns within large data sets. Computing power is now cheap (historically speaking). Data has proliferated and the cost of data storage has also fallen dramatically. Taken together, those conditions are ripe for the development of artificially intelligent tools that can take even more repetitive tasks off the desks of lawyers.

The rise of data science and AI within the legal industry is a potentially profound development. Firms will need to think much more strategically about the nature of their work, what can and should be done by people (vs what can and should be done by machines), and how the resulting work product should be priced.

Legal analytics

As noted above, in-house legal departments are investing in new capabilities focused specifically on operational improvement. As Peter Drucker noted, "If you can't measure it, you can't improve it". Legal operations professionals are serious about metrics and have included legal analytics and other metrics in their rubric of "core competencies".

If clients are getting serious about measuring law firm (vendor) performance, firms themselves better get serious about it too. That means adopting legal analytics – and knowing how your firm is performing – before your clients have already measured your performance and found it lacking in some important way.

All of these information management issues are related by the common thread of capturing data, analyzing that data in ways that enable firms to deliver greater value to clients, and improving processes to capitalize on the insights gained from those analyses. The good news is that an entire ecosystem of companies has emerged to help both law firms and their clients with KM, AI, data science, and legal analytics. The key for readers is to incorporate that into your broader strategic thinking.

Disaggregation of legal processes

Like knowledge management, a great deal has already been written on the topic of legal process outsourcing (LPO) and alternative legal service providers (ALSPs). In some circles the term has become synonymous with offshore services for document review and other elements of the legal process. Likewise, the term historically focused primarily on the litigation process, with little attention given to transactional practices. The rise of e-discovery technologies has helped to remind law firms that outsourcing options includes a robust group of domestic companies and firms.

Thomson Reuters' Legal Executive Institute teamed up with Georgetown University Law School to research the ALSP (and by default LPO) market in late 2017. They found that the global market for ALSPs had grown to $8.4bn (still a relatively small fraction of the estimated $700bn global legal industry). The work of ALSPs has expanded well beyond document review and e-discovery services.

Although LPO and ALSPs are becoming more commonplace and more widely accepted (expected in some circumstances), there are a number of considerations that make LPO a continuing strategic issue for law firms. Those considerations include the following.

Ethical and professional standards

The American Bar Association's guidance related to LPO underscored that outsourcing (including offshoring) should be subject to the same ethical requirements as domestic use of non-lawyer services. That would include:

- Supervising LPO vendors' work (attorney and paraprofessional);
- Preserving all client confidences (inclusive of attorney-client privilege);
- Avoiding conflicts of interest (i.e. the vendor must avoid conflicts in essentially the same manner as the originating firm);
- Generally bill only for the direct cost of outsourcing (i.e ABA considers it to be unethical to bill those services at a mark-up that would reflect in-firm servicing of that work); and
- Ensuring client consent as the matter dictates.

Client relationship management

In addition to the ethical considerations associated with LPO (most of which are focused on the attorney-client relationship), there are additional considerations relative to the impact LPO can have on relationships. For instance, given the broader trend toward disaggregating the legal process among larger institutional clients, a strong capability for managing ALSPs and strong relationships with LPO vendors can become a real positive in selected client relationships. Further, firms or practices pursuing a co-creation of value approach (see chapter 9 on value innovation tools) would likely include LPO alternatives in the mix, and transparency regarding the advantages, drawbacks, and costs of various options would be part of any conversation with clients. Most broadly, LPO can and should be considered one means of increasing the value clients obtain for the fees invested in legal services – thereby strengthening the relationship.

Trade-offs and lost capabilities

Legal process outsourcing, like other forms of outsourcing, can lead to a permanent loss of capability in the area of activity the firm elects to outsource. That is true whether the outsourcing involves human activity (document review) or technology support (e-discovery technology). The outsourcing decision involves making strategic trade-offs. For instance, outsourcing document review means that work is no longer available for the training and development of new associates. Likewise, outsourcing e-discovery technology to a third party vendor means that capability is never developed and owned within the firm. Those may in fact be wise trade-offs. However, having made those trade-offs, it can prove to be very difficult to bring those activities back in-house to the firm.

Captive ALSPs

In some respects the term "captive ALSP" is oxymoronic. However, the Thomson Reuters/Georgetown study[2] identified ALSPs captive as subsidiaries to several law firms including Wilmer Hale, Clifford Chance, Eversheds, Orrick, Allen & Overy, and Reed Smith. Many of these captives work for other firms as well as their owners – particularly if they are stringent in avoiding conflicts and sit in a distinct operational entity. One can even envision captive ALSPs being a joint venture of two or more major law firms who want greater control of the outsourced activities and related revenues, but want to minimize investment and risk (in fact, early examples of joint investments by law firms are already emerging). Does a so-called linoleum floor operation (captive as a subsidiary) make sense strategically? It probably does for some firms.

Risk management and professional liability

Finally, regardless of who owns the ALSP vendor and where it is located (onshore or offshore), firms that outsource work will need to have solid risk management policies and procedures in place. The bar has underscored the importance of supervising work performed by vendors. Expect legal liability insurers to ask questions as well – and perhaps to exclude certain risks or ask for additional premiums to cover risks associated with outsourced work.

Business development and marketing

Business development and marketing is an issue both extensively covered and well supported within law firms – as well as by intelligent professional associations such as the Legal Marketing Association. A thorough treatment of the subject is beyond the scope of this book. Yet, it cannot simply be passed over in the context of the major strategic issues law firms face in the coming years.

Two aspects of law firm business development and marketing are especially important for those embarking on strategic planning. First, a great deal of law firm marketing investment is made to advance firms' brands – branding in the context of law firm marketing is a critical strategic issue. Second, business development and cross-marketing are a recurring topic in law firm strategic planning processes – a strategy that is both alluring and vexing. Each will be discussed and framed below.

Brand building

Both Acritas and BTI Consulting run large-scale law firm brand indices focused on who the leading brands are in the legal industry. Their lists are not identical (the methodologies differ somewhat), but there is tremendous overlap (70 percent of the firms on Acritas' top 20 list are in the BTI "brand elite"). Those findings are not terribly encouraging for most law firms vis-à-vis brand awareness. In terms of brand awareness and favorability, both lists are overwhelmingly dominated by the largest and most profitable firms in the US.

This should not be surprising on any number of levels. Those firms have the deepest pockets from which to invest in their brands (it essentially costs a larger firm less per partner to invest in awareness building, since they spread that investment over more partners). Further, those firms are generally the most visible firms from a public relations standpoint as well (more closed deals, more big cases, more partner awards, more promotions and hiring announcements, etc.). Advertising executives know that brand building requires frequency and reach (i.e. you have to tell a lot of people about your brand, over and over again, to have an impact on awareness and favorability).

In addition, the survey findings underscored an important reality facing law firm marketers. The legal industry – despite all the mergers and combinations – remains a highly fragmented industry. Even the biggest and most well-resourced law firms – those at the very top of the brand rankings – are only truly reaching a small percentage of institutional clients (never mind the vast middle market).

Given these insights regarding the advantages of scale in brand building, the continued fragmentation of the legal marketplace, and the reality that most firms lack sufficient resources to purchase enough advertising frequency and reach to truly build brand awareness, some consideration needs to be given to how best focus market building resources. Ansoff's 2x2 matrix[3] (see Figure 5) is a good guide for this purpose.

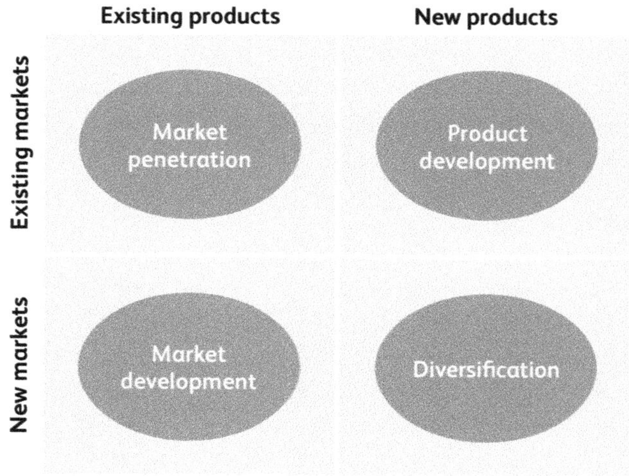

Figure 5: Ansoff's 2x2 matrix.

Ansoff and others have reached several conclusions applying this matrix to commercial enterprises (including professional service firms). First, there is generally not enough growth focusing strictly on selling the same services to existing clients – in fact, there is usually some drop-off in revenues if a law firm focuses solely on this activity. Second, there is a high probability of success in taking "new" services to existing clients – essentially, cross-marketing (more on this below). Third, market development is most successful when a firm focuses on taking established expertise and existing strengths to new clients and new markets – in areas where there are strong references, third party ratings of excellence, and other accolades. Finally, taking unproven services to new markets is a high risk approach with low probability of success.

Applying these insights to marketing and branding would suggest spending market development resources on the strongest practices in the firm – rather than on unproven services or general image advertising. General image advertising is hampered by the fragmentation of the marketplace and limitations on resources. Spending on unproven service areas is subject to low probabilities of success.

One final caveat with regard to the branding issue – namely, these insights are not arguments against investing in becoming community leaders in the market(s) the law firm is resident. There is real value in taking leadership roles in community and civic organizations, on arts boards, at the local legal aid society, and with effective social service agencies. That activity is more costly in terms of partner time than in sponsorship dollars. Not only does that type of investment help with general brand building for the law firm, it is also the right thing to do.

Business development and cross-marketing

Following up on the Ansoff matrix above, business development activities should focus primarily on existing clients. Certainly, some resources must be invested in maintaining existing relationships and the work that goes with them – including baseline client entertainment (lunches, sporting events, etc.). More importantly, resources need to be invested in expanding the range of work the firm does for existing clients.

Heidi Gardner led a research team at Harvard Law School to look at collaboration. The results of that research were published in *Smart Collaboration* (Harvard Business Review Press, 2016).[4] The biggest finding was that when multiple partners and practices work with a client, the size of the relationship multiplies (it is not just adding on work, it multiplies work). Her team also found that clients who work with more partners and more practice areas are much more likely to continue using a law firm. The more extensively a client knows and uses a firm, the more likely it is that the relationship will endure into the future.

The primary obstacle to effective cross-marketing is partner willingness to introduce other areas of practice and/or other partners to "his" (or her) clients. That can be a function of partner compensation systems (a potential loss of origination credit or poor cooperation among partners wrangling over credit). It might be resisted as an imposition on partner autonomy. Further, it might be resisted because the partners lack confidence or trust in other practice groups – they fear their relationship will be soured by poor service quality.

Ultimately, the best opportunities for marketing and business development success are in two areas: 1) investing in exposing the firm's strongest practices and people to new clients and markets; and 2) introducing new services to existing clients. A judicious balance between these two areas is the best way to grow revenues and profit across the entire firm. Inject those insights into your firm's strategic planning.

References

1. For survey data on AFAs see the Altman Weil Law Firms in Transition annual survey at www.altmanweil.com/lfit2018/.
2. For information on the Thomson Reuters/Georgetown University study on Alternative Legal Service Providers please see https://store.legal.thomsonreuters.

com/law-products/solutions/legal-outsourcing-services/outsourcing-insights/alternative-legal-service-provider-study-2017 (registration required).

3. Ansoff, I: "Strategies for Diversification", *Harvard Business Review*, Vol. 35 Issue 5, Sep-Oct 1957, pp. 113-124.
4. Gardner, Heidi: *Smart Collaboration*, Harvard Business Review Press (2017).

Chapter 7: Strategic planning tools and principles

The previous chapters provided a roadmap for carrying out strategic planning in a law firm setting – primarily at the firm level, but also at the practice group level. Those chapters referenced a number of strategic planning tools, techniques, and principles. Some of the most powerful and useful planning tools, analytical frameworks, and underlying principles will be covered in this chapter.

In the short sections that follow, five strategic management tools and principles will be explained in the context of law firm strategic planning. In most cases, the sections will provide:

- Background information describing the origins and implications of the tool or management principle;
- A "how-to" primer on applying the tool or principle in a law firm context; and
- Additional reference information for those looking for in-depth (often book length) treatments of the topic.

The five tools/management principles examined in the sections that follow are:

1. Portfolio analysis;
2. Product lifecycle management;
3. Competitive intensity (the five forces);
4. Scenario based planning; and
5. The balanced scorecard.

1. Portfolio analysis

Portfolio analysis (and portfolio management) traces its origins to the leading management consulting firms of the 1960s and early '70s. There were several variations on the same underlying idea; namely, that the key to effectively managing a business with multiple product lines and/or multiple divisions was to understand the role each should play in the company's overall strategy.

Further, each approach to portfolio analysis examined products or business units from two fundamental perspectives. First, they looked at the relative competitive position of the business or product line. Second, they assessed the market in which that business unit or product competed.

Origins of the tool

Perhaps the simplest version of portfolio analysis was the Boston Consulting Group's (BCG) growth-share matrix. In the BCG version of portfolio analysis, relative competitive standing was measured via market share. The model assigned considerable value to being the market leader. The growth rate of the overall market for the product (or business unit) was the principal measure of market attractiveness.

The BCG growth share matrix came complete with colorful terms for businesses or products in each quadrant of the matrix – some that are still in use today. For instance, businesses with leading share in fast growing markets were called "stars". Business units or products with a leadership position in slower growth or mature markets were "cash cows". Lagging businesses in slow growth markets were "dogs". The underlying principle suggested that "cash cows" fund the development of the next wave of "stars" – and companies should divest from "dogs".

Arthur D. Little, McKinsey and Company, and other strategy consulting firms developed more nuanced and flexible approaches to portfolio analysis. Those approaches allowed for a more tailored approach both to assessing relative market position (not just a function of market share) and to assessing market attractiveness (more than simply a function of market growth). The resulting portfolio assessment, however, yielded a similar set of generic prescriptions for the role various business units should play within the overall portfolio.

Law firm application

The application to law firms – particularly general practice business law firms – should be quite apparent. As law firms have grown, developed multiple practice and industry specialties, and become more managerially complex, the need to apply some order to that increased complexity has grown. Portfolio analysis and portfolio management provide a set of tools well designed for precisely this type of organizational complexity.

Essentially, practice groups (generally including industry groups) are in most respects like a strategic business unit in a diversified corporation. They offer distinct services, have unique underlying "production" or operational capabilities, face identifiable competitors, and compete in markets that differ (sometimes dramatically, sometimes subtly) from the markets of other practices. Further, it is entirely possible (in fact advisable) to measure the financial performance of a practice group – if not on a fully loaded profit and loss basis, then certainly on the basis of contribution to firm profits (e.g. revenues net of direct expenses before the allocation of firm overhead).

Further, given the inherent limitations on resources, it is not feasible to treat every practice the same. Nor is it sensible to expect the same results and contributions from every practice. Some practices are well suited to attract new clients to the law firm. Some are well positioned to drive profitable revenues. Some are integral to maintaining a deep and lasting relationship with clients. Ideally, a firm should be able to define its expectations of each practice based on a portfolio analysis – and the practices should be able to pursue a valuable role within the firm in response to those expectations.

Using and applying the tool in a law firm setting

Chapter four provided an abridged description of how to apply portfolio analysis tools in a law firm setting. That chapter was primarily focused on explaining how best to approach the broader range of trade-offs and choices facing a firm during the strategy development phase of the planning process. Portfolio analysis is a great tool for informing the trade-offs that need to be made relative to practice group roles and expectations.

However, that chapter only provided a cursory explanation of how to work through questions of relative market attractiveness and relative market position. This section provides a bit more depth for those intending to use portfolio analysis as part of their strategic planning process

Portfolio management is a straightforward process in which management (or a strategic planning committee) ranks practices along two critical dimensions – the *attractiveness of the market* in which the practice group competes; and the *relative market position/strength* of the practice group. Each of these dimensions is discussed in more detail below.

Market attractiveness

The attractiveness of any given market is a function of a variety of factors – some purely objective, others more subjective. The key to using the portfolio analysis tool is to agree on a consistent set of "attractiveness factors" and each factor's relative importance.

Some examples of market attractiveness factors follow:

- **Competitive intensity** influences the attractiveness of a market. Highly competitive markets may not be as attractive as those with less competition. Note that a separate tool designed for assessing competitive intensity is discussed in some depth in a subsequent section below.
- **Rate sensitivity** is an issue in many legal market segments. Markets or specialties that do or can bear premium billing are clearly more attractive than those with a high degree of rate sensitivity.
- **Market growth** is another obvious factor in rating the attractiveness of markets. Patent litigation was attractive throughout the 1990s and 2000s in large part because of the consistent growth in that market – since the passage of the America Invents Act, IP litigation has declined and become highly competitive.
- **Market size** must also be considered. A large market is generally more attractive than a small one. A large, growing market is even better.
- **The needs and demands of the firm's existing client base** is usually a factor. For instance, if virtually all of the firm's corporate clients need and use the firm's tax services, the tax market would be rated favorably on this particular factor.

Other factors might also be included in this analysis, such as historical or future profitability; regulatory and other external influences on the market; and the technology required (now and in the future) to compete effectively in the market.

Relative market position/strength

The other dimension to consider in a portfolio analysis is the relative market position of each practice group. The key word is relative – to key competitors and to the needs and expectations of the market.

Again, a variety of factors determine the relative market position of a practice. Some examples follow:

- The relative quality of lawyers and/or work produced is a key factor, but is often difficult to rate objectively. Third party ratings can serve as a proxy here (e.g. number of attorneys listed in Leading Lawyers or tier ranking in Chambers).

- Practice financial performance (measured by contribution, realization, revenue per lawyer, net income per partner, or other means) can be an indication of relative market strength. As noted above, profit potential can also serve well as a factor in determining market attractiveness.
- Market reputation/perception can be a strong indication of a practice's relative strength. Is the practice considered the leader, among the leaders, at parity with most firms, lagging other firms, etc.?
- Market share – locally, regionally, or nationally – is another key measure of relative market strength. Unfortunately, law firms generally have to rely on the number of lawyers they have in a given area as a surrogate for market share. Nevertheless, share and share growth are good measures of relative market position.

Plotting the portfolio

Assessments of each practice group's relative market position and the attractiveness of the practices' respective markets can be viewed graphically by juxtaposing the two dimensions (market position and attractiveness) on a matrix. At a basic level, market attractiveness and relative market position ratings can be broken down to three "generic grades" – high, medium, and low.

The result is a three by three matrix as shown in Figure 6.

		Market attractiveness		
		High	**Medium**	**Low**
Relative market position	**High**	Invest and grow	Invest and grow	Maintain pursue/ premiums
	Medium	Invest and grow	Maintain	Maintain or divest
	Low	Improve to survive	Improve or divest	Exit

Figure 6: Market attractiveness and relative market position.

A practice's position on the matrix provides direction on what strategies are appropriate for that practice group. The following points briefly describe these strategic implications:

- **Highly attractive, high relative position** – clearly the best of both worlds, this situation calls for aggressive investment and growth. In fact, others will envy this position and defensive strategies are also appropriate as the practice group expands on and consolidates its position.
- **Highly attractive, medium relative position** – this situation also warrants a growth-oriented strategy. However, an additional challenge is added in that the practice group also needs to find ways to improve on key factors that influence its relative market position.
- **Highly attractive, low relative position** – this situation poses a potential trap. The market is clearly attractive, but the firm's practice is a relatively weak player. In product markets, companies will try to double their market share in relatively short order or quit the market. Likewise, firms need to determine key milestones for practice improvement and move on if those milestones are not reached.
- **Moderately attractive, high relative position** – this situation warrants growth and investment. The practice's market position may also allow for relatively aggressive pricing and high profitability.
- **Moderately attractive, medium market position** – a solid practice in a mature market can and should be maintained and well managed. A well-executed maintenance strategy can yield satisfied clients and healthy profits for years.
- **Moderately attractive, low relative position** – if improvements cannot be made relatively quickly, a practice in this situation should be phased down.
- **Low attractiveness, high relative position** – while the market may not be attractive, the practice's strong position likely warrants a maintenance strategy. Furthermore, premium rates and premium clients should be pursued by a practice in this position.
- **Low attractiveness, medium relative position** – if the practice can be maintained profitably, do so. If not, a phased withdrawal is called for.
- **Low attractiveness, low relative position** – exit this market.

The matrix suggests relatively generic strategies. Naturally, the specific strategies a firm should pursue depend on many factors, some of which reach well beyond the scope of this analysis. Nevertheless, portfolio management is an extremely valuable tool in making resource allocation decisions among practices.

Applying the tool

Using the portfolio management tool is simply a matter of applying the above factors in a consistent, objective manner. Steps in applying portfolio management are described in the following.

- **Decide what you are going to analyze**. Agree on which (if not all) practice areas you will analyze and across how broad a market (local, regional, national). Be consistent across the entire analysis.
- **Define market attractiveness factors to be used**. Agree on which factors will be used to determine market attractiveness for each practice (e.g. rate sensitivity, market growth, market size, etc.).
- **Agree on relative weights for each factor**. All factors are not created equal. For instance, market size and growth may be more important to the firm than overall competitive intensity. Agree on a weighting system for the attractiveness factors.
- **Score each practice in the firm's portfolio on the attractiveness factors**. Objectively rate each practice against all factors. Use the same scale for all practices. Be consistent. The result will be a weighted measure of the attractiveness of each practice's market.
- **Define relative market position factors to be used**. Agree on what factors truly measure the relative market position of the firm's practices (e.g. relative quality, market share, reputation, etc.).
- **Weight the factors**. Again, all factors are not created equal. Quality may be much more important than market share.
- **Score each practice on the relative market position factors**. Again, be objective and consistent in rating the practices. The result will be a weighted measure of each practice's relative market position.
- **Plot the two scores on a matrix**. Each practice will have two scores – one for market attractiveness; the other for relative market position. Plot them on a matrix like the example below, where 10 is the highest score and 1 is the lowest (or simply high, medium, and low).

This tool can be applied with greater or lesser degrees of sophistication, depending on the circumstances facing a firm and the information available to it.

Additional reading

Portfolio management is covered well in numerous management and marketing text books. Philip Kotler and Gary Armstrong's (Kellogg School of Business, Northwestern University) *Principles of Marketing*, now in its 17th edition, is among the better sources.

David Aaker (Amos Tuck School of Business Administration, University of California) also covers the topic well in *Developing Business Strategies* (John Wiley and Sons, 1984).

2. Product life cycle management

Product life cycle management is an analytical and predictive tool that helps firms to understand what strategies can or will work in light of the relative maturity of a service offering and the related market. It is based on extensive research on the history of product and service markets. While services and products can and do diverge from the traditional life cycle, it is such a common experience in business that a fundamental understanding of the principle is critical to effective strategic management.

Origins of the tool

Research into the growth and development of multiple markets in the post-World War II era underscored the consistency of product life cycles across multiple markets. The fundamental principles guiding product life cycles indicate four consistent phases:

1. **Introduction**. While specifics vary, the introduction phase of a new product or service is generally marketed by low volumes, high production costs and high prices. The buyers in the introduction phase are so-called early adopters – customers or clients who are indifferent to price because they are enamored by the appeal of the new product or service. Beyond the early adopters, any other potential clients require extensive education to understand what the product or service is and how it could benefit them. Success is far from certain in the introductory phase and there are typically very few firms capable of delivering the new product or service;

2. **Growth**. Sometimes referred to as the "rapid growth phase", this portion of the product life cycle is marked by rapid market acceptance of the new product or service. Competitors (some innovative in their own right, others simply imitators) multiply to capitalize on the rapid growth evident in the market. As volumes grow quickly, prices tend to fall – however, the cost of production and/or overall efficiency improves quickly as well. Because demand is growing quickly and competition is still highly fragmented, the growth phase is usually very profitable for successful competitors;
3. **Maturity**. Eventually growth slows considerably (or stops all together) and market demand reaches a stable plateau. The product or service is widely accepted at this point, so volumes are relatively high at the mature plateau. Competition becomes better organized, consolidation takes hold in many markets, and the stronger competitors establish segmented positions (e.g. high quality/differentiated, low cost, etc.) to ensure sustainable margins that fit their business model and cost structure; and
4. **Decline**. Ultimately, products and services will slide into a decline phase. Generally, decline sets in when a better alternative emerges. However, other influences can trigger decline as well (for instance, the global ban on CFCs). In some markets, the decline is slow and the strongest competitors sustain a profitable business for years. More often, only niche players and very low cost providers remain in declining markets as profit opportunities evaporate.

This description is the most basic and widely accepted view of the product life cycle. Some authors have refined the concept to include a developmental stage (i.e. a stage prior to commercialization of the product or service), some have split the growth phase into early and late stages (there are subtle differences between early and late stage growth), and some overlay technology adoption cycles onto the product lifecycle.

Graphic depictions of the product life cycle are widely available. QuickMBA.com provides a helpful and generic example, as illustrated in Figure 7.

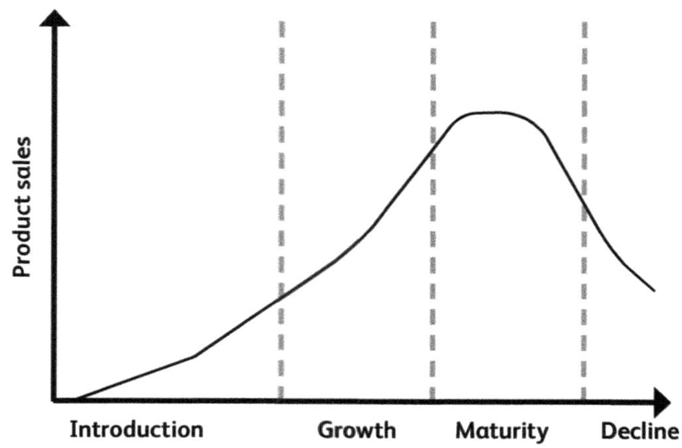

Figure 7: The product lifecycle. Source: QuickMBA.com.

Law firm application

The majority of legal services are in an extended maturity phase. There are many competitors and profitability is acceptable. Firms and practices have staked out market positions that fit their broader reputations and cost positions.

The broader applicability to law firms is fairly evident, but consider some examples to help illustrate the value of understanding the phases of product life cycles and applying them to a selected legal market or legal service.

Some of the strongest and most profitable firms attained real and sustained advantages by being the first movers in the introduction phase. Skadden Arps was an early leader in hostile takeovers. Wachtel Lipton introduced the poison pill defense. Chadbourne & Parke got an early lead in global project finance. There are real advantages to being a first mover – but you rarely hear about the thousands of hours invested in ideas that never find a client. For law firms, the best introduction phase markets are those that respond to an unfulfilled need of deep-pocketed clients (e.g. investment banks, Fortune 100 corporations, high net worth individuals, etc.).

Rapid growth phases emerge in legal markets quite frequently – and on occasion last for more than a few years. Energy related markets have witnessed rapid growth and the entry of multiple competitors in several segments (e.g. renewable energy in the desert southwest (solar) and Midwest (wind), natural gas in Appalachia, off shore oil (multiple instances), etc.). Intellectual property (especially patent) litigation had a long period of rapid growth before plateauing in the late 2000s. Firms that capitalize on this growth and that apply their strengths to those new service markets benefit significantly.

As noted above, most legal markets enjoy years of stability and maturity. However, mature markets do, over time, face margin pressures. Law firms need to be able to differentiate (to capture the high value segment of a mature market) or reduce costs to maintain reasonable profitability. As one clear example, employment law and employment litigation risks are increasingly underwritten by insurance companies – serving that market requires a low cost operation to service the insurance segment or differentiation to service companies who remain "self-insured".

Ultimately, legal markets do go into decline. At times this is entirely predictable. For instance, when tax laws changed regarding the treatment of losses in real estate (and other) syndications, it was clear a previously profitable service was going to die – some exited, some innovated (moving to Real Estate Investment Trusts), and some were shocked by the sudden over capacity in their real estate practices. Other times the decline is slower and less obvious.

Three phases of the process played out over the past few years in the IP marketplace in the US. Following passage of the America Invents Act, a new set of procedures were created to allow individuals and companies to challenge the validity of issued patents. Only the most sophisticated IP boutiques and practice groups carried out these proceedings in the earliest days. By 2013-14, rapid growth emerged as many validity challenges were filed. IP litigators who initially referred these proceedings to specialty firms entered the market. By 2017 the market had matured, many firms were filing and defending validity challenges at the US Patent and Trademark Office, and prices became considerably more competitive. It will likely be years before the market declines, but the mature market place is already segmenting.

Using and applying the tool in a law firm setting

Using the insights offered by the product life cycle in a law firm setting does not lend itself to step-by-step instructions. However, there are basic insights and principles that can and should be applied at the practice group level:

- **Bigger risks/bigger rewards**. Early entrants – the innovators – take on the most risk and make the biggest up-front investments. But, when a new service innovation finds a clientele, there is generally very little price sensitivity. Further, the reputation for leadership and innovation typically stays with the firm and the practice long after others enter the market;

- **Ready profits in the growth phase**. Recognizing a growing market and pursuing it aggressively is a solid path to profitable revenues. If your firm has the fundamental capability to serve a rapidly growing market, invest in marketing and business development there;
- **Maturity requires segmentation**. Once demand stabilizes, understand where your firm and its practice best fits in the mature market. Are you well suited to defend a particular segment? Are you a lower cost player who should pursue volume growth? Are you a highly differentiated competitor who can afford to focus on the highest end of the market?
- **Recognize decline and pick a strategy**. Historically, three strategies have proven effective in declining markets. Some can retreat to a niche that remains solid (or may even be growing, counter to the rest of the market). Some should stop investing in the market, maximize near term cash flows, and gradually exit (transitioning people to other growing or mature markets). Some pursue the low cost position and work to force higher cost competitors out of the market (essentially consolidating capacity).

Further reading

Like portfolio analysis, the product life cycle is well-researched and has been written about widely. It is covered in nearly every graduate business school. R. Preston McAfee covered product life cycles (along with other fundamental tools and principles) well in his book *Competitive Solutions: The Strategist's Toolkit* (Princeton University Press, 2002).

3. Competitive intensity – five forces analysis

Competitive intensity is a function of more than the direct competition among rival firms. It is strongly influenced by several other factors. By examining all the forces influencing a market, important insights can be gained vis-à-vis how challenging the competitive environment is and is likely to be in the future.

Origins of the tool

Michael Porter highlighted the idea of analyzing "five forces" directly influencing the competitive intensity of any given market or industry in his 1980 landmark book *Competitive Strategy*. Porter noted that the intensity of competition is most obviously influenced by the ongoing rivalries among direct competitors. However, he also pointed out that this direct rivalry was insufficient as an explanation for why competition is so much more intense in some industries than in others.

Porter pointed to five direct influences on competitive intensity (see Figure 8).

1. **Direct rivalry**. Naturally, the direct rivalry among competitors has a significant influence on competitive intensity. Porter pointed to a range of characteristics that will make direct rivalry more or less intense. For instance, high fixed costs, lack of differentiation (e.g. commodity products), over-capacity, and fragmented competition will all lead to more intense direct rivalry (see the graph for more examples).
2. **Supplier power**. Industries or markets in which suppliers have significant bargaining power often lead to higher levels of competitive intensity. For instance, personal computer makers have relatively little bargaining power against Microsoft – they need an operating system and Windows is the industry standard (with notable exceptions).
3. **Buyer power**. Likewise, industries or markets in which customers have out-sized bargaining power are generally more competitively intense. For instance, automotive parts manufacturers are at a severe bargaining disadvantage vis-à-vis their large, global customers. Since the great recession, clients have gained substantial bargaining power over their law firms.
4. **Threat of substitutes**. Markets that face ready substitutes are generally more competitively intense. For instance, the rise of online news sources has created a difficult to overcome substitute to taking a daily newspaper.
5. **Threat of new entrants**. Finally, the presence or lack of barriers to entry in a market can strongly influence the intensity of competition in an industry. For instance, there are relatively low barriers to new real estate brokerage firms entering any given market – creating a constant check on competition in that market.

With the rise of technology – and internet-based products, services, and markets some authors (see McAfee) have noted the rise of a sixth factor influencing competitive intensity – the presence (and importance) of complimentary products or services. For instance, both iPhone and Android smartphones benefit from the presence of thousands of complimentary applications ("apps").

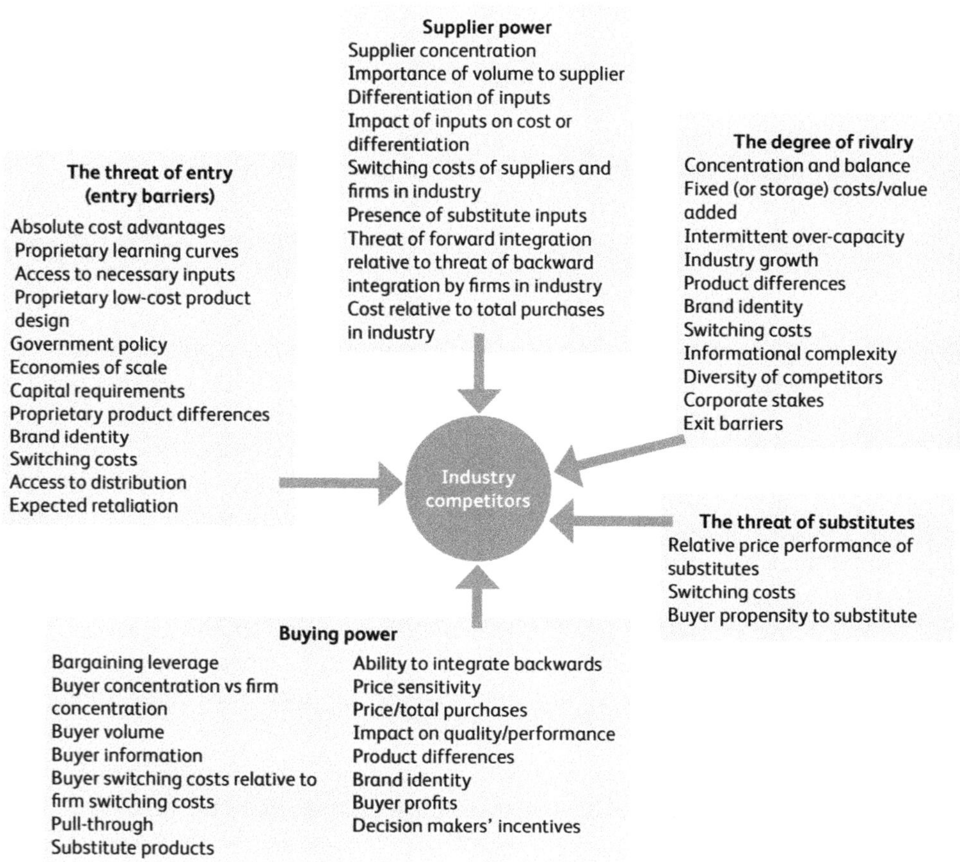

Figure 8: Porter's five direct influences on competitive intensity.

Law firm application of the tool

The tool is most useful for law firms analyzing the likely competitive intensity of markets for particular practice groups and/or specialties. A high level thought process would include the following considerations:

- **Existing rivalry** is usually well understood. Third party rankings can provide a degree of objectivity to the process. Because law firms are necessarily open regarding capabilities, a review of rivals' websites can provide additional insight into the actual capabilities of competitors. Further, Peer Monitor and other peer benchmarking services can provide insights into prevailing rates and cost structures among rivals;

- **Supplier power** is generally weak in the legal industry (the run-up in associate starting salaries throughout the 2000s notwithstanding). Landlords in most markets are anxious to attract law firm tenants. Other vendors are similarly anxious to attract law firm clients (with the possible exception of very small firms). Law schools are producing ample "raw materials". The only real exception to this general rule is the bargaining power of lateral partners (with a book of business);
- **Buyer power** is clearly growing in the legal industry. Several markets have already been directly influenced by bargaining power (e.g. insurance defense, patent prosecution, employment litigation, etc.). This is a factor that should be carefully assessed when considering competitive intensity in any given legal market;
- **The threat of substitutes** is strong in some markets (e.g. tax compliance, government relations, etc.). However, in most areas there are few substitutes for effective legal counsel; and
- **The threat of new entrants** is a growing one to some specialty areas. The industry remains fragmented. Good lawyers do form new firms – often taking a collection of strong people with them. Thus, so-called micro-boutiques have emerged in patent prosecution, pushing rates down in the process. Litigation boutiques and contract attorney services create increased intensity in some markets. The potential for legal process outsourcing is a form of new entry as well.

Further reading

The best source regarding five forces analysis is the original author – Michael Porter's *Competitive Strategy* (Simon & Schuster, 1980). A simple Google search will also turn-up literally dozens of informed discussions on the topic.

4. Scenario-based planning

Scenario-based planning enables a planning team to think systematically about the future and the implications the future holds for the firm. The process focuses on the major drivers of the future (sometimes referred to as "megatrends"). By researching those drivers, developing insights into the potential directions they can take, and the probability of those directions emerging, a reasonable outlook can be developed.

By linking the reasonable (or highly probable) outlooks regarding all the major drivers, alternative future market conditions can be outlined. The idea is not to predict the future per se, but rather to highlight plausible potential futures (two or three alternative views of the future). Each future scenario carries its own set of implications for the firm. In turn, those alternative scenarios can help to inform vision development and direction setting.

Origins of the tool

Scenario planning was initially developed for the US Military by Herman Kahn. Kahn went on to form the Hudson Institute and also implemented versions of scenario based planning at the RAND Corporation. Those early applications of the tool were intended to inform large scale, long range planning at the Pentagon.

Royal Dutch Shell and Pierre Wack are generally credited with popularizing the use of scenarios in a business setting. Shell began using scenarios in the early 1970s, which provided important and useful insights regarding the potential for oil shortages – and potential responses Shell could take to those shortages. The first oil crisis in the early '70s intensified Shell's commitment to scenario based planning and the company credited scenario planning for its superior management throughout the second oil crisis in the late '70s.

Peter Schwartz has written most extensively on the topic since the 1980s. Schwartz and his partners in the Global Business Network have championed a robust approach to scenario planning – combining extensive research with executive judgment (relative to assigning probabilities to future outcomes).

Today, scenario based planning is most commonly used in times of intense and uncertain change. Companies facing fundamental change in their industries and/or deep uncertainty regarding the future find scenario planning to be extremely helpful in charting a strategic direction that will enable the company to succeed – regardless of what the future actually holds.

Application of the tool to law firms

The tool is most useful to law firms in the vision development and strategic direction setting phase of the planning process. Assuming the firm prepares a relatively thorough background analysis in Phase I of the process, developing future scenarios for use in strategic planning is not particularly onerous. It does require an additional round of analysis using that background data, but it yields potentially unique insights – and depending on the culture of the firm, it can be a fun and engaging exercise for people.

Using and applying the tool in a law firm setting

The process steps for using and applying the scenario based planning tool in a law firm setting build on the analyses and background research outlined as Phase I – Situation Analysis (chapter 2). It is an interim step that is used to inform and drive Phase II – Setting Strategic Direction (chapter 3).

Scenario development in a law firm setting involves the following steps:

1. **Agree on scenario drivers**. The process begins by agreeing on the major drivers of the firm's (and its market) future. That generally yields a list of eight to 12 drivers, including things like demographic trends, the competitive landscape, industry consolidation technology trends, client trends and preferences, and so on.
2. **Driver research and forecasts**. Relying primarily on the data gathered for Phase I, a summary of the major trends influencing each driver are compiled. Logical potential directions each driver might take over the next ten years are also developed and described. The results of this work can be documented in white papers if the planning team is willing to invest time learning more about the drivers of the future.
3. **Craft alternative scenarios**. Using the driver research as a guide, two or three plausible alternatives are crafted describing the future environment the firm will encounter in ten years. Those scenarios should present a gestalt view – weaving together all of the drivers. Note that in most cases some drivers are highly predictable (e.g. demographics), while others may vary significantly and in a non-linear fashion (e.g. future regulation). It is helpful to name each scenario, both to provide a shorthand tool for the planning team and to highlight the core theme(s) of the scenario.
4. **Consider implications**. Finally, the process turns to considering the implications each scenario holds for the firm. Used as a tool in the early stages of Phase II, that process can be used to envision

a vision, mission, and set of primary excellence goals that would enable the firm to thrive regardless of which scenario emerged. In other words, the planning team works to identify a vision and goals that are positive and powerful in every circumstance.

Further reading

Peter Schwartz provides a detailed approach to scenario development in his book *The Art of the Long View: Planning for the Future in an Uncertain World* (Doubleday, 1991). Schwartz's approach is more involved than necessary, but it is an excellent overview of the process.

More recently, Bruce MacEwan (aka Adam Smith, Esq.) published a book of possible future scenarios for law firms, *Tomorrowland* (self-published and available on Amazon). It is a handy shortcut to future scenarios facing mid-size and large law firms, ranging from "nothing changes," to profound dislocations brought on by macro level trends in the legal industry.

5. Balanced scorecard

As noted earlier in chapter 5, the balanced scorecard is a comprehensive tool for managing strategy implementation on a continuing basis. That chapter highlighted a basic "how-to" approach for applying balanced scorecards in a law firm setting – that material will not be repeated here.

That chapter did gloss over both the benefits and challenges associated with adopting the balanced scorecard in a law firm setting. This section summarizes the key benefits and challenges associated with pursuing a balanced scorecard approach to implementation management.

Benefits and advantages of balanced scorecards

Business research has demonstrated two very important conclusions regarding the balanced scorecard. First, organizations that adopt and utilize the balanced scorecard as an integrated system improve their own performance and out-perform organizations that do not use an integrated scorecard. Second, organizations that have adopted the balanced scorecard experience much higher levels of buy-in and understanding vis-à-vis the organization's vision and strategy – they understand what it means to them on a day-to-day basis.

Law firms are late to the table with regard to adoption of the balanced scorecard. As case studies demonstrate, firms have tended to focus on elements of the scorecard and have not yet taken an integrated approach to the process. Yet, in considering the potential benefits of adopting an integrated approach, the nature of the opportunity becomes apparent. Those potential benefits include:

- Development of clear linkages between the work of the firm and its practices, with high level goals directed toward improved profit per partner;
- Dramatically improved implementation of firm-level and practice-level strategic plans;
- Pointed improvement in performance associated with each dimension of the balanced scorecard:
  - Especially on behalf of clients and in the development of the capabilities of a firm's people;
  - But also in the development of other important capabilities (e.g. the use and application of technology) and in business processes; and
- Substantial improvement in practice group performance – where the integrated nature of the balanced scorecard can be best leveraged in the context of the common clientele, service offerings, skill base, and work processes that exist at the practice group level.

Potential challenges in adopting a balanced scorecard approach

The potential benefits of employing the balanced scorecard in a law firm environment are substantial. However, the nature of the tool can clash with the historic structure and culture of many sophisticated law firms. There are meaningful challenges to implementing the balanced scorecard in a law firm. While the degree to which these barriers exist in any given firm will vary, law firm management should be aware of these potential challenges before embracing the balanced scorecard for their own firm.

Shareholders are service providers and client relationship managers

A basic assumption of the balanced scorecard is that shareholders are passive investors seeking competitive returns on their investments. In the overwhelming majority of law firms, by contrast, the shareholders (partners) are also active in delivering services, developing client relationships, and managing the firm and its practice groups. Owners are not passive investors in the enterprise.

Taken as a whole, the parallel roles partners play as owners, as service providers, and as business getters, create a complicating factor never accounted for in Kaplan and Norton's original conception of the balanced scorecard.

Resistance to business process focus

Focusing on business process in a law firm often creates a backlash against what is characterized as "cookie cutter approaches to the law". Standardized processes do not sit well with highly trained professionals who see nuance and a need for variation in every client matter. In addition, standardization can be perceived as impinging on partners' (and other attorneys') autonomy vis-à-vis choosing an appropriate course of action on any given client matter.

Potentially conflicting incentives

In many areas of practice, billable hours are directly related to the revenues that practice generates. Growth over the past two decades has often been driven by clients' needs. In litigation departments there was a real need to provide scale in order to respond to the volume of documents involved in the discovery process (accelerated more recently by e-discovery). On the transactional side of the practice, the speed and complexity of many transactions had similarly driven a need for scale.

That need for scale (and by definition for hours) had been a boom for law firms. However, particularly in the context of the rise of information technology, clients are more apt to be looking for greater efficiency rather than greater scale. That has the potential to create conflicting incentives in a balanced scorecard context.

More generically, so long as the billable hour remains a fundamental driver of how law firms are paid for their services, there is a potential for conflicting incentives between clients' desire for greater predictability and/or efficiency and shareholders' desire for growing PPEP.

Partner compensation systems

An important potential challenge to the adoption of balanced scorecards in a law firm involves the alignment (or lack thereof) of the partner compensation system with the overall strategy of the law firm and its practice groups. In a perfect world, a firm's partner compensation system would be well aligned with its strategic priorities. The reality is that compensation systems are often lagging indicators of the strategic direction a firm has embraced.

Difficulty of measurement

Quite simply, some things are hard to measure – at both a macro (firm or practice) level and/or at a micro (action plan) level. People oriented goals are notoriously difficult to surround with quantitative metrics that actually relate to the qualitative goals the firm is attempting to achieve.

Cultural issues

Finally, cultural issues can be a challenge to the use of balanced scorecards in some law firms. Some firm cultures actively resist the type of accountability associated with the balanced scorecard. Namely, balanced scorecards tend to focus accountability on doing what you said you were going to do. Partners in particular can become accustomed to not following through on action plans – so long as they bring in clients and bill sufficient hours.

Similarly, some firm cultures limit the management authority of firm and/or practice group managers. Major decisions are often taken via democratic processes. Partner compensation systems focus on relatively few hard measures (e.g. origination, billable hours, etc.). Management simply does not have the authority to require partners to engage in action planning and metric development.

Further reading

Two sources are potentially valuable to those seeking to adopt a balanced scorecard approach to implementation management. First, of course, Norton's and Kaplan's original text is extremely valuable (*The Balanced Scorecard: Translating Strategy into Action*; Harvard Business School Press; 1996). In addition, the ARK report *Balanced Scorecards for Law Firms* (2009) provides an in-depth discussion of how to implement the tool in a law firm setting.

Chapter 8:
Value innovation tools and techniques

Most of the strategy tools and principles discussed in the last chapter focus on competitive strategy. That is, the tools and techniques focus on competitive positioning, competitive intensity, and/or execution of competitive strategy.

In 1997, Clayton Christensen published *The Innovator's Dilemma*, which led to the emergence of research and methodologies focused less on competitors and competitive strategy and more directly on creating new sources of demand, new customers, and entirely new markets. In addition to Christensen's (and his colleagues') work on disruptive innovation, other approaches to creating new demand and/or creating new business models emerged throughout the 2000s. Those include Co-creation (Prahalad and Ramaswamy, *The Future of Competition: Co-Creating Unique Value with Customers*, 2004), Blue Ocean Strategy (Kim and Mauborgne, *Blue Ocean Strategy*, 2005), and the Business Model Canvas (Osterwalder and Pigneur, *Business Model Generation*, 2010).

Bryan Leavy at Dublin City University Business School uses the term "value innovation" as an umbrella to talk about these newer strategy models. He notes that their distinction from more traditional competitive strategy concepts can be summarized in four points (*Strategy & Leadership*, 2010 and 2018):

1. These models view the basic strategy challenge as creating and capturing new demand;
2. They put the primary emphasis in strategy development on the customer, rather than the competition;
3. They recognize the potential for new demand, captured from "non-consumers"; and
4. They aim for a leap in value through business model innovation (i.e. changing the game).

The balance of this chapter focuses on outlining these value innovation tools and techniques – and exploring how they can be applied in a law firm setting.

Disruptive innovation

Disruptive innovation is an approach to product, service, and business process development that focuses on delivering "good enough" products or services. In other words, disruptive innovations target and capture the so-called low end of a given market – usually by delivering "good enough" performance at a dramatically lower price than full service or full function incumbents.

Disruptive innovators typically attract either non-consumers of a product or service (essentially creating a new solution and a new market) and/or customers who are "overshot" or over-served by a higher cost and higher function solution than they really need (creating a low-end disruption). There are dozens, if not hundreds, of examples of disruptive innovations entering and capturing the low end of their given market – Skype instead of full function video links, Quicken rather than more complex accounting software, cameras integrated into cell phones, and Metro's free daily newspapers.

Origins of the tool

Clayton M Christensen is credited both with the research that identified the fundamental principles of disruptive innovation – in the first of two landmark books, *The Innovator's Dilemma* – and with the subsequent work that codified how to pursue disruptive innovation in your own organization. Christensen's second book, co-written with Michael Raynor, *The Innovator's Solution*, outlined the steps to pursuing disruptive innovation.

The disruptive innovation process involves three major steps:

1. **Opportunity identification**. This step includes identifying non-users of a product or service as well as users whose needs appear to be "overshot". With potential target clients or customers in mind, opportunity identification focuses on identifying the "jobs to be done" for those customers (i.e. identifying through traditional market research the core needs those non-users and overshot users actually need fulfilled).
2. **Idea formulation and shaping ideas**. The second step involves developing disruptive ideas – the authors provide a range of

supporting tools to help with that process. With ideas in hand, this stage of the disruption process calls for an iterative process for refining and testing ideas. Christensen's research found that innovators rarely understand the needs of non-users or overshot users out of the gate. Rather, they need to refine their ideas via low cost, low risk failures – leading to a refined product or service that can capture a larger and potentially growing market.

3. **Building a business**. The third step focuses on establishing a sustainable business to market the solution and grow the business to reasonable scale. This stage requires the innovator to identify and understand critical areas of uncertainty, experiment in ways that resolve that uncertainty in the early growth stages of the business, and refine the underlying business model in response to what is learned.

Christensen and his co-authors have built upon and refined this approach over the past ten years and there are now a number of industry-specific innovation methodologies in circulation (though none focused directly on the legal market).

Application to the legal industry

The application of disruptive innovation in the legal industry is largely two-fold. First, for well-established firms, understanding disruptive innovation is important. In particular, successful low-end innovators can and will dramatically alter an established market – client relationships, pricing expectations, profit potential, and otherwise. Ultimately, they often surpass incumbent competitors – fundamentally changing the market they undercut initially.

Second, there may be markets ripe for disruption that can be served by your own firm. In those instances, firms or practice groups can directly apply the disruptive innovation tools to targeted markets – identifying non-users/overshot users; defining the "jobs to be done" for them; creating, testing, and refining solutions; and building a sustainable business that grows to scale over time.

Examples of disruptive innovation in the legal industry have emerged in a number of specialty areas, as well as in specific aspects of larger scale legal processes. For instance, the emergence of pre-paid legal services and "do-it-yourself" wills have captured clients who were previously non-users of legal services (note that in some cases, those non-users turn out to be high net worth individuals with substantial legal needs, initially attracted by a pre-paid solution). Likewise, talented patent attorneys have created micro-boutiques that do nothing but patent prosecution on a fixed fee per application basis. Further, legal process outsourcing shops are creating dramatically lower cost approaches to selected tasks in the discovery phases of large-scale litigation.

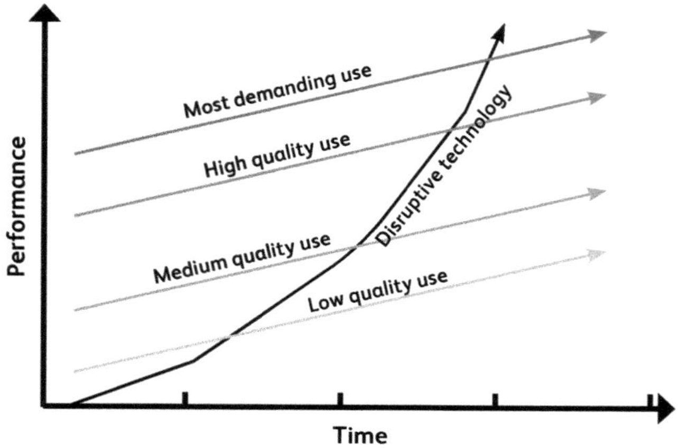

Figure 9: Disruptive technology.

It is critically important to understand the underlying business models of emergent disruptive innovators. If their solution is scalable, if it can add new capabilities over time (gradually encroaching on your practice's incumbent solution), and/or if it attracts clients who perceive themselves to be "overshot", those innovators need to be taken into account in the context of developing and implementing competitive strategies.

Using the tool in a law firm setting

The three-phase approach outlined above applies fairly universally. It is certainly applicable in a law firm setting without unique tailoring or embellishment. Because there is considerable depth, nuance and insight in *The Innovator's Solution*, it is recommended that those planning to pursue disruptive innovation take the time to read that book and use the many supporting tools provided in that text.

There is an important consideration law firm leaders should recognize prior to engaging in an all-out pursuit of disruptive innovation. Michael Raynor continues to research disruptive innovation with a high level of energy. His book, *The Innovator's Manifesto*, includes an important insight for incumbent competitors. Namely, incumbents tend to be highly successful at creating incremental innovations (i.e. innovating at the high end), but are dramatically less successful in introducing disruptive innovations (see Figure 10).

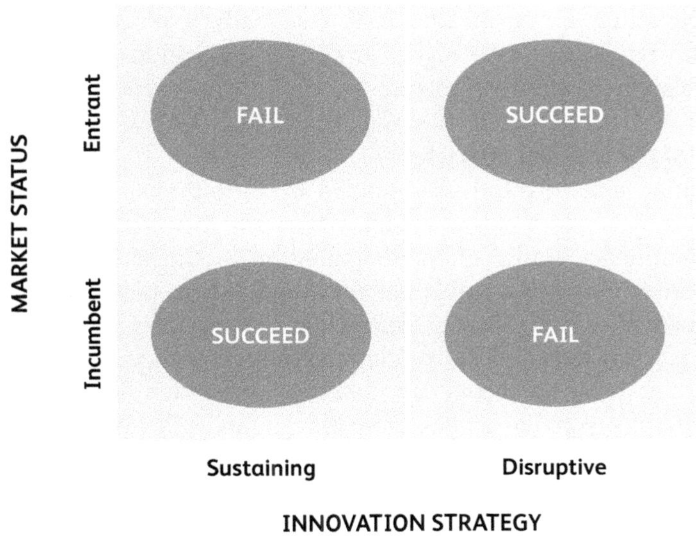

Figure 10: Incumbents vs entrants.

This would suggest that firms wanting to capture disruptive innovation in an area where they are already an incumbent competitor should consider a couple of alternatives to directly pursuing disruption within their firm/practice group. First, they can acquire a growing disruptor – someone who has already worked through the first two (and possibly all three) stages in the disruptive innovation process. Second, they can set up an ancillary business to develop the disruptive service offering – removing some of the principal barriers incumbents face when trying to launch disruptive innovations that will compete with their well-established services.

Further reading

Those interested in pursuing disruptive innovation (or who have a strong interest in the topic) are encouraged to read Christensen's and Raynor's *The Innovator's Solution* (Harvard Business School Publishing, 2003). Raynor's new book, *The Innovator's Manifesto* (Crown Business, 2011) provides valuable insights into the drivers of success and failure among innovators.

Co-creating unique value with customers

Disruptive innovation provides a process and roadmap for creating low end solutions that fundamentally alter established markets. Co-creation is a process for creating high end solutions that have unique and enduring value for customers. It is essentially a process for taking premium practices to ever higher levels of value and for strengthening client relationships in the process.

Origins of the tool and principles

Co-creation emerged and was defined by C K Prahalad and Venkat Ramaswamy – both professors of business at the University of Michigan. They identified a number of foundational shifts in the nature of relationships between businesses and their customers – shifts that alter how and where value is created. Those shifts include growing access to information on the part of clients; globalization regarding viewpoints and perspectives (i.e. not only do clients have increased access to information, that information is global in scope); networking among clients (for example, via the Association for Corporate Counsel, LinkedIn, and other formal and informal networks); and a willingness to experiment – particularly with digital and/or information driven products and services.

Given that backdrop, Prahalad and Ramaswamy found that increasingly value was created at the point of interaction between businesses and their clients. Value was becoming less a function of creating a product or service to be purchased (i.e. take it or leave it). Rather, value was being created as businesses and their customers created unique solutions together.

For many in the legal industry, this insight is not particularly novel. Because legal services often require dynamic interaction and unique tailoring of solutions via direct interaction with clients, the idea of co-creating value is a standard operating practice for many lawyers. Because Prahalad and Ramaswamy approached this dynamic from a mass market, product-oriented perspective, they were able to develop some basic principles that are potentially valuable to law firms.

Law firm application

Law firms can adopt co-creation tools and principles quite readily. It is a natural extension of how most practices and practitioners approach the delivery of services already. Specifically, attorneys are used to interacting with clients and tailoring solutions to the unique needs, objectives, and circumstances those clients face.

Co-creation tools simply provide a roadmap for taking that interaction to a higher level – recognizing that the world has become more interconnected and information is more readily available to clients than it has been in the past. By recognizing and embracing that change, more value can be created for clients and, in the process, relationships can be strengthened.

Using the tool in a law firm setting

Applying co-creation in a law firm setting involves embracing four fundamental, ongoing principles in client interactions:

1. **Dialog**. Dialog means interactivity, engagement, and a propensity to act – on both sides (client and law firm). Beyond simply listening to clients, dialog suggests shared learning on the part of two problem solvers.
2. **Access**. Access focuses primarily on providing access to information and tools. For instance, many firms have implemented extranets and/or cloud-based solutions for managing shared information with clients. Embracing the access principle takes that one step further, ensuring access to the insights, knowledge, and other foundational tools the law firm uses on behalf of clients.
3. **Risk assessment**. To fully engage in co-creation, clients need to have a deeper understanding of the risks (and trade-offs) they face when selecting and creating a particular solution. Some attorneys are extremely good at helping clients assess risk and make wise choices – others are not. Helping clients assess risk is fundamental to co-creating value.
4. **Transparency**. Historically, there has been a natural imbalance regarding some elements of the relationship (e.g. pricing, underlying costs, profit margins, etc.). Some of that imbalance has already broken down. For instance, starting salaries for associates are published openly at NALP and profit levels are openly reported in the AmLaw 200 rankings. The transparency principle calls on firms to continue and expand that openness.

While many will object to (or fear) the level of openness called for by the principles above, that fear is generally unsubstantiated in actual practice. Clients do not object to their law firms earning a healthy profit – they understand that profitability is the cost of doing business into the future.

Furthermore, because they are actively part of key decisions regarding the creation of solutions and the management of risks, the value received relative to the fees charged is generally perceived to be very high.

Co-creation works most effectively when complexity is high and resulting solutions are genuinely unique and of high value. In those high-end settings, law firms are well served adopting principles of co-creation. They are natural extensions of long-standing tradition and lead to deeper, stronger, and more loyal client relationships.

Further reading

Co-creation is covered in great depth in Prahalad's and Ramaswamy's book *The Future of Competition: Co-Creating Unique Value with Customers* (Harvard Business School Press, 2004). Interviews with Professor Prahalad and condensed (article length) perspectives on the topic are available in *Strategy & Leadership* (Emerald Publishing, Vol. 32, No. 3, 2004 and Vol. 34, No. 2, 2006).

Blue ocean strategy

Disruptive innovators focus on over-served markets – providing "good enough" solutions at the low end of a market, thereby drawing in new buyers and disrupting the existing market. Co-creators work directly with customers to create tailored solutions with unique value. Blue Ocean Strategy focuses on uncovering new ways to aggregate demand, redefining or creating new categories in the process.

Origins of the tool and principles

Professors W Chan Kim and Renee Mauborgne published *Blue Ocean Strategy* (Harvard Business School Press) in 2005 based on work they began together in the late 1990s. The central idea was to focus strategy on finding so-called "blue oceans" where there was no real competition since the market was yet to be created. They contrasted this to "red oceans" that represented market spaces that were already crowded and competitive (i.e. "bloody").

As an example of Blue Ocean Strategy in practice, the authors highlighted Cirque du Soleil. The creators of Cirque du Soleil eliminated selected elements of a traditional circus (such as animals), added elements of theatrical performance (story arc and choreography), and tapped a previously non-existent market.

Kim and Mauborgne summarized the change in mindset and philosophy as illustrated in Figure 11.

Red Ocean	Blue Ocean
Compete in the existing market	Create uncontested market space
Beat the competition	Make competition irrelevant
Exploit existing demand	Create/capture new demand
Make the value/cost trade-off	Break the value/cost trade-off
Choose: Low cost or differentiation Then align to that strategy	Pursue both differentiation and low-cost position

Figure 11: Red ocean and Blue ocean philosophies.

In the most successful Blue Ocean innovations, costs are reduced or eliminated in areas traditionally thought to be integral to value delivery. At the same time, value is added in areas that were previously under appreciated or not present at all. The methodology encourages innovators to look at the sources of value in a market and take active steps to "eliminate–reduce–raise–create" value (the "four actions framework"). To continue the Cirque du Soleil example, Kim and Mauborgne outlined a four actions framework as shown in Figure 12.

Eliminate Star performers Animal acts Aisle concession sales Multiple show arenas (three-ring circus)	**Raise** Unique venue
Reduce Fun and humor Thrill and danger	**Create** Theme Refined environment Multiple production Artistic music and choreography

Figure 12: Four actions framework: Cirque du Soleil.

Since publishing, *Blue Ocean Strategy* interest in applying the methodology to a variety of businesses and markets has been high. Kim and Mauborgne published a practical, hands on, "how-to" approach in *Blue*

Ocean Shift in 2017. That book outlines a five-step process, similar to what was described in the original book. However, the authors added insights related to building a "blue ocean mindset" into an organization and provided a process structure that addressed the challenges associated with engaging people in creating and pursuing blue oceans.

Law firm application

The application of Blue Ocean Strategy in a law firm does not require a special variation on the tools and methods outlined by Kim and Mauborgne. However, it may prove to be more difficult to implement in a law firm environment, simply because there is a high level of resistance to eliminating or reducing elements that have traditionally been seen as a source of value.

The Blue Ocean Strategy team recently published a law firm case study that provides insights into both the promise and the challenge of embracing a blue ocean approach in a law firm. Their client, central Asian law firm Centil (offices in Kazakhstan, Kyrgyzstan, Uzbekistan, and Tajikistan), was competing in a fiercely price competitive market with both local law firms and international firms. Centil took a unique approach to the market, using the four actions framework.

Eliminate Hiring "star" lateral attorneys	**Raise** Hiring younger, "undervalued" lawyers Government interaction Quality of English language content
Reduce Specialized products and services Legal events as marketing initiatives	**Create** Economic advisory unit London office Online platform where clients and prospects can get "free advice"

Figure 13: Four actions framework: law firm application.

The full case study can be found at www.blueoceanstrategy.com.

Using the tool in a law firm setting

Taking a blue ocean approach to strategy in a law firm setting involves three main components:

1. Adopting a "blue ocean perspective". Kim and Mauborgne outline cognitive traps that should be avoided to create the right mindset

(e.g. focusing on existing clients, confusing technology pioneering with value innovation, treating the exercise as niche creation or segmentation, etc.).

2. Utilizing the market creating tools the authors and their team outlined in *Blue Ocean Strategy* and refined in *Blue Ocean Shift*. Those tools and the related process involve five major steps (outlined briefly below).
3. Ensuring the firm takes a "humanistic approach" to the entire process. Kim and Mauborgne saw that the most successful blue ocean teams "recognized people, acknowledging their fears, their insecurities, their need to be treated with dignity, their desires to matter". At the core, the humanistic approach involves engaging people directly in the innovation process.

The five-step blue ocean process requires a substantial investment of time and energy (including 'adopting a blue ocean perspective'). The steps are treated at book length in the authors' books. So, the points below should be considered simply an introduction to a much richer body of knowledge.

Step 1: Getting started:

- Select the right (inclusive) team for the blue ocean innovation process.
- Assess the current innovation pipeline and project portfolio grouping ideas into three categories:
- Pioneers = Value innovators;
- Migrators = Value improvers; and
- Settlers = Value imitators.

Step 2: Understand where the firm is now:

- Apply Kim and Mauborgne's "Strategy Canvas" to assess what the current value drivers are (i.e. what dimensions are competitors focused on today); and
- Identify and agree on the need and potential for a shift in the entire value curve.

Step 3: Imagine where the firm could be:

- Discover the pain points of buyers imposed by the current shape of the value curve (i.e. the trade-offs buyers are forced to make); and
- Identify the total demand landscape you can unlock across three tiers of non-clients:
  - "Soon-to-be non-customers" who are looking for alternatives;
  - "Refusing non-customers" who have looked at the offerings of competitors and rejected them; and
  - "Unexplored non-customers" whose needs have generally been considered to belong to other industries (e.g. Southwest Airlines converted people from buses and cars).

Step 4: Find a route to get there:

- Apply six paths to reconstructing market boundaries:
  1. Look across alternative industries;
  2. Look across strategic groups within your industry;
  3. Look across chains of buyers;
  4. Look across complementary products and services;
  5. Rethink the functional-emotional orientation of the industry; and
  6. Participate in shaping external trends over time.
- Apply the four-action framework (e.g. eliminate, reduce, raise, create) to define a new value curve (and new business model).

Step 5: Make your move:

- Select preferred strategies, conduct rapid market tests, and refine the business (similar to what Christensen described in *Innovator's Dilemma*);
- Refine and invest in the newly formalized business model; and
- Scale up the new business/product/service.

Further reading

Readers are strongly encouraged to reference either *Blue Ocean Strategy* (Harvard Business School Press, 2005) and/or *Blue Ocean Shift* (Hachette Books, 2017).

For a good article length treatment of *Blue Ocean Shift* readers can turn to Brian Leavy's Masterclass article on the topic in *Strategy & Leadership* (Vol. 46 Issue: 3, pp.10-20).

Business model canvas

Unlike the three value innovation approaches outlined above, the business model canvas is less an innovation methodology and more a managerial discipline. The canvas provides a logical framework for evaluating new (or existing) business models and optimizing that business model – improving the probability of success in the process.

Origins of the tool and principles

The business model canvas was introduced by Swiss professor and strategist Alexander Osterwalder in 2008 (just as the global economy was entering a prolonged and deep recession). Osterwalder teamed with Yves Pigneur (professor of management information systems at the University of Lausanne). The tool essentially emerged from Osterwalder's Ph.D. work studying under Professor Pigneur.

The tool is effectively a nine box "canvas" on which innovators or business model evaluators examine crucial elements of the business model.

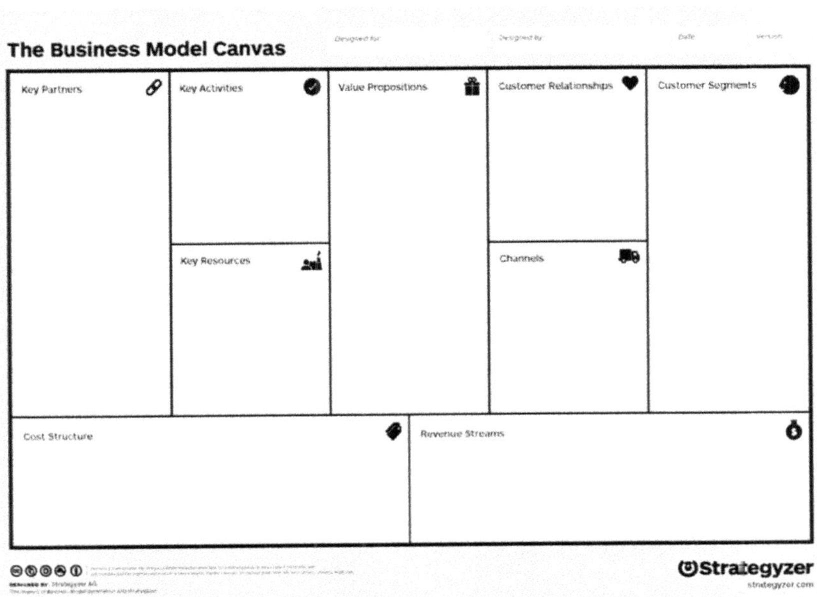

Figure 14: The business model canvas.

At the center of the canvas is the value proposition.

- What does the business do to meet the needs of its customers in a way that distinguishes it from competitors? In some respects, the value proposition aligns with Porter's concept of generic strategies (i.e. winning by being cheaper/lower cost, winning by being differentiated, etc.); and
- Value can be delivered through a wide variety of benefits (e.g. performance, customization, design, brand, price, cost reduction, accessibility, convenience, etc.).

To the left of the value proposition are elements central to the business' infrastructure. There are three specific "infrastructure" elements in the business model canvas:

- Key activities – the most important activities in executing a company's value proposition (e.g. production, network alignment, problem solving, etc.);
- Key resources – the resources that are necessary to create value for the customer (e.g. physical capital, human capital, intellectual capital, etc.); and
- Key partners – the relationships that make the value proposition feasible or that help to optimize the delivery of value (e.g. suppliers, complementary products and services, outsourcing partners, etc.).

To the right of the value proposition are elements focusing specifically on customers and their needs. There are three customer-oriented elements in the business model canvas:

- Customer relationships – the type of relationship the company wants to create with targeted customer segments (e.g. personal assistance, self service, automated services, communities, co-creation, etc.);
- Customer segments – the segment(s) of the market the company wants to serve (e.g. mass market, niche, diversified (multiple niches/segments), etc.); and
- Channels – the route a company takes in order to deliver its products or services to customers (e.g. its own channels, partner channels/distributors, or a combination of both).

The entire business model canvas rests on two financial elements:

- The cost structure of the business must be well defined and understood:
  - Is the company going to be cost driven (reducing costs relentlessly) or value driven (focused less on costs than on creating perceived value)?
  - What traditional aspects of cost structure apply to the business (e.g. can it capture economies of scale, does it have high fixed costs, etc.)?
- The revenue sources similarly have to be well defined. Is the business selling assets/products, services (fee for service models), access (streaming services)?

With analysis and data in hand, a team can complete a business model canvas on a set of flip charts in relatively short order. By seeing the entire business model on a single page, elements can be challenged, modified, and refined – strengthening the business model as a whole in the process.

Law firm application

With the rise of alternative legal service providers (many captive to law firms), the business model canvas has never been more relevant to law firms. The model can obviously be applied to any practice group or service offering. It can also be applied to stand-alone (or quasi-stand-alone) business units a firm may be attempting to stand-up to compete in the marketplace.

For instance, if a firm decided that it wanted to start an e-discovery subsidiary to serve both its own and other law firm's e-discovery project needs, the business model canvas would provide a healthy managerial discipline for evaluating that business. Does the proposed business have a value proposition? Which customers and segments will it be serving? What infrastructure will it have in place (e.g. key relationships, key resources, etc.)? Critically, what cost structure and revenue streams will the business have to ensure it is a sustainable business?

Using the tool in a law firm setting

Osterwalder created an open-source venture to extend the business model canvas to whomever wants to use the tool. Most resources are free to use at Strategyzer.com and the team there has created a number of complementary tools as well (e.g. value proposition canvas). Many companies have joined a community at Strategyzer to access training programs, canvases and other tools, consulting assistance, and other content.

The tools are literally free to use in a law firm setting. As noted above, a team can put the business model canvas on the wall and using post-it notes, address all the key questions raised by the nine elements across the canvas. Further, the team can work collaboratively to refine and improve the business model in a workshop setting before making hard dollar investments.

Further reading

Readers are encouraged to reference Osterwalder and Pigneur's book *Business Model Generation* (Wiley & Sons, 2010). Osterwalder's Strategyzer website www.strategyzer.com also offers a wealth of information in exchange for basic contact information.

Case study 1:
Intellectual property boutique, efficient director involvement – Sterne, Kessler, Goldstein and Fox

Note: This case study was published in winter 2011 – an update on Sterne, Kessler, Goldstein & Fox follows this original case study.

Sterne, Kessler, Goldstein and Fox (Sterne Kessler) is a relatively large intellectual property boutique based in Washington, DC. The firm has roughly 150 fee earners and 100 attorneys – including over 50 PhDs in a range of hard sciences. The firm was founded in 1978 and leadership and management have largely transitioned to the second generation of directors.

When the firm decided to begin developing a new strategic plan, there was a clear bias toward finding ways to directly involve and engage all directors in the planning process. However, there was a parallel realization that: 1) the firm had grown substantially and the director group was now larger; and 2) the directors (in fact, all fee earners) were extremely busy and their involvement needed to be gained as efficiently as possible.

Preparation and process design

As a means of balancing efficiency and active director involvement, the firm's leadership team – the managing director, the chief operating officer, and the chief financial officer (in collaboration with the executive committee) – designed a process that would keep the planning process moving, while engaging the full directorship at several junctures. The process relied on three interlocking groups to maintain momentum and involvement. The leadership team (i.e. managing director, COO, and CFO) took responsibility for analytical and other "leg work" that could be done offline. A steering committee of well-respected equity directors took responsibility for drafting elements of the strategic plan and related implementation plans as the process unfolded. Finally, the full directorship was directly engaged at key points throughout the process.

The firm began the planning process with some key background information-gathering steps already completed. First, the firm had completed an extensive (and strategy oriented) client survey less than a year prior to starting the planning process. In addition, the firm had very solid financial analysis and trend data – at the firm, practice group, and individual levels – already in hand (in part due to ongoing work by the CFO and in part due to special projects completed by a senior business analyst).

Fact-gathering and background analysis

Because important baseline information was already available regarding client perspectives and financial trends, the fact-gathering phase was relatively streamlined. All equity directors were interviewed in one-on-one sessions to gather initial input regarding the state of Sterne Kessler, market opportunities and threats, major trends in the IP marketplace, and strategic issues. A parallel set of focus group interviews were conducted with cross-sections of income directors and associates.

Major trends identified in the interviews were further investigated and facts were gathered to enhance the firm's understanding of those issues. That included multi-year trend lines on patent, copyright, and trademark applications and grants by technical field. It included an extensive review of trends in IP litigation (cases filed, parties to those cases, settlement values, and trial awards). It included trend line reviews of *inter partes* cases before the US Patent and Trademark Office (USPTO) and cases before the International Trade Commission (ITC).

All of that information was digested into a single foundation report for strategic planning purposes. The findings were shared in writing with all partners. Those findings were discussed in more depth at an extended directors' luncheon meeting (substituting the strategic planning material for the regular agenda that month).

This approach allowed all directors to have direct involvement at two key stages of the background development phase – providing initial input regarding issues and trends, and reacting to and discussing the implications of the findings of all background analyses. The rest of the analytical work was managed efficiently by the leadership team.

Direction setting and strategy development

The direction setting and strategy phases of the process benefited most directly from the process design in terms of moving quickly and efficiently, while maintaining director involvement.

The leadership team designed an agenda for direction setting and strategy development that spread the work over two long half-days (essentially, the afternoon and evenings of two consecutive days). Ideas for vision and primary excellence goals were framed in advance, so the steering committee would not have to begin discussions from an entirely blank slate.

The steering committee developed rough drafts of the vision, values, and purposes, as well as an initial set of primary excellence goals. The steering committee took the further step of identifying the likely or logically implied strategies that flowed from each of the initial primary goals. That initial work concluded the first day (and evening).

The leadership team used the morning of the second day to refine the rough drafts and advance the work the steering committee had done on strategy development. The steering committee then reconvened for another long half-day (beginning with a working lunch and again working into the evening). That session produced a more complete draft strategic plan, as well as a number of agreed upon implementation priorities to accompany that plan.

The leadership team further refined the draft plan and related implementation priorities for presentation to the full directors group. That offline work included creating a document for directors to review prior to the meeting, as well as a set of slides designed to elicit discussion and feedback at the meeting itself.

The direction-setting and strategy development phase ended with a meeting of all directors. The draft plans and related implementation priorities were discussed at length, ideas for further refinement and implementation implications were identified, and next steps were agreed upon to complete implementation planning and begin implementation.

Implementation planning and closure

Implementation planning involved three distinct sets of activities. Firm level implementation initiatives were fleshed out by the leadership team. That work benefited from the earlier input of both the steering committee and the directors as a whole. The leadership team also developed templates to help the firm's practice group leaders develop implementation plans for their respective groups. Finally, the leadership team designed an equity directors' retreat agenda to bring closure to the process and ensure every equity director had a direct role in strategy implementation.

Implementation at the practice group level built on the preparation of the leadership team. Each practice group leader, assisted by the firm's strategy consultant, used the implementation planning templates and leadership team advice to build simple and direct plans for practice-level implementation of selected strategies. Although the practice groups worked from common templates, each group's implementation initiatives and priorities were customized to the unique characteristics of their group and their groups' clientele.

The directors' retreat provided an opportunity for all directors to review and provide feedback on the firm level and practice level implementation plans. It also provided a direct opportunity for each director to embrace specific role(s) and accountabilities for strategy implementation. At the conclusion of that retreat, all directors had affirmed their agreement with the strategic direction and had embraced specific roles in the implementation of that strategy.

Subsequently, the strategic plan has had a high level of visibility within the firm. It was the central theme of a firm-wide retreat the year after its adoption. And, it has driven much of the positive growth and development at the firm and practice levels.

Update

The strategic plan discussed in the case study above was adopted in early spring 2010. Since that time, the author has joined Sterne Kessler as chief marketing officer, with responsibility for strategy development and coordination at the firm, practice, and individual level; marketing and business development; market analytics and competitive intelligence; pricing and related project budget management; and client planning and value management.

Implementation and results from initial strategy

The 2010 strategic plan centered on five primary excellence goals. The firm has made substantial, measurable progress relative to each one of those primary goals.

One primary goal focused on market leading patent preparation and prosecution – this primary goal built on an existing strength for Sterne Kessler. Among the firm's accomplishments in this area since adoption of this goal are the following:

- The firm developed a state-of-the-art docketing system, including one of a kind "double docketing", ensuring key USPTO and other deadlines are accurately managed;
- That system was improved and extended to a secure mobile app that the *Financial Times* named the "most innovative law firm technology" in 2016;

- The firm and its partners are widely recognized for market leadership in patent prosecution (e.g. "Band 1" in *Chambers and Partners*, "Tier One" in *Intellectual Asset Management (IAM)*, "Highly Recommended" by *IP Stars (Managing Intellectual Property)*, etc.); and
- The firm has adopted a number of tools that have helped improve both the timeliness and efficiency of patent prosecution at Sterne Kessler.

A second primary goal focused on building a well-integrated litigation practice. This goal formalized (and built consensus for) a strategy the firm had begun pursuing in the 'aughts.

- The firm grew its litigation practice via a combination of lateral and entry level hiring;
- In addition, a number of directors and associates with litigation experience committed themselves fully to litigation (district court, USITC, and appellate);
- *Inter partes* work (all forms of litigation) expanded from roughly 15 percent of revenues in 2009 to nearly 50 percent in 2017 – a period of time during which overall revenues grew more than 60 percent firm-wide; and
- The firm and its leading practitioners are increasingly recognized by the same third party rating and ranking organizations noted above for leadership in IP litigation.

A third primary goal focused on capturing a position of "thought leadership" in the world of IP law. This also built upon a historic strength of the firm, based on feedback from clients in 2009.

- The firm's directors were sought out for input and advice as the America Invents Act (AIA) of 2011 was debated and signed into law;
- The AIA created an entirely new set of patent validity proceedings at the USPTO via a Patent Trial and Appeal Board (PTAB). Sterne Kessler's directors wrote the first book on so-called *PTO Litigation* (Thomson Reuters); and
- Since creation of the PTAB in September 2012, Sterne Kessler has perennially ranked first or second for number of proceedings at the PTAB.

A fourth primary excellence goal focused on ensuring deep relationships with clients. This goal recognized the potential power of a point discussed in chapters outlining the first two phases of the planning process. Namely, the best strategies create alignment and synergy across the primary goals.

- By committing to the other three goals above (strong prosecution, growing litigation, and thought leadership), Sterne Kessler had a tremendous opportunity to do more with and for its clients; and
- Sterne Kessler has more than doubled the number of seven-figure clients it serves – a useful metric for the scale and depth of client relationships.

The final goal focused on people and culture. Like several of the goals above, it was an opportunity to build on an existing strength.

- Sterne Kessler has been voted (by its people in blind surveys) a "Best Place to Work" by both the *Washington Post* and the *Washington Business Journal* several years running since adoption of the 2010 strategic plan;
- Attorney headcount has grown by roughly 30 percent while total revenues have grown over 60 percent, improving productivity and profitability; and
- Profitability increased over 60 percent even while the directorship has expanded significantly.

Strategy updates and looking forward

Over the past several years, Sterne Kessler has launched a number of initiatives driven by the direction set in the 2010 strategic plan. As the market and the firm evolved, new initiatives helped to sustain positive momentum and capitalize on emerging market opportunities. Among the initiatives the firm launched to drive the strategy forward were the following:

- Both the *PTO Litigation* book initiative (repeated in a second edition in 2017) and the larger push to provide thought leadership in anticipation of and in response to the AIA reflected a large scale and coordinated initiative across the firm – both by its fee earners and by its professional staff;

- The firm's life sciences practices developed a coordinated strategy to balance growth in its patent prosecution and PTAB litigation work on behalf of biotech and pharmaceutical innovators, with growth in life sciences litigation; and
- The firm has launched a number of technology and/or industry focused initiatives, contributing to leadership positions in nanotech, industrial biotechnology, biosimilar product development, and automotive electronics.

Most recently, all directors worked with the leadership team to update the primary excellence goals. The new strategic plan simplifies the direction somewhat – moving from five to four primary goals. The direction now includes an active commitment to maintaining a balanced, full service IP practice (patent prosecution, trademark and anti-counterfeiting, litigation across all IP venues, strategic advice, and opinions of counsel).

More information is available on the firm's website at www.sterne-kessler.com.

Case study 2: Mid-size firm, governance driven process – Clark Hill

Note: This case study was published in winter 2011 – an update on Clark Hill follows this original case study.

Clark Hill (at the time of writing the first edition) is a roughly 200 attorney law firm with roots in Michigan and offices across that state, in Chicago, Washington, and Arizona. At the time that Clark Hill pursued the planning process outlined below, it was a roughly 90 attorney firm with offices in Detroit, Birmingham (suburban Detroit), and Lansing (Michigan's state capital).

The firm was the product of a successful merger between two 100-year-old firms. Organized as a PLC, Clark Hill had a five-member executive committee elected by the members (one person, one vote) in staggered three-year terms. The executive committee in turn elected the firm's CEO. The firm's COO reported to the CEO and was charged with leading all administrative functions of the firm on a continuing basis. On balance, firm leadership was relatively young (for instance, the oldest elected member of the executive committee was 48).

Clark Hill's "bread and butter" clients at the time of the planning process were successful, closely held middle market companies – mostly in Michigan. That said, the firm had attracted work from Fortune 100 companies – including some of the very largest headquartered in the state.

Preparation and process objectives

Prior to embarking on a full scale strategic planning process, Clark Hill's members reached general agreement on a long-range direction for the firm. That direction called for the firm to be more growth oriented – open to creating a larger regional footprint and a "brand" that reflected growth orientation.

Prior to launching the planning process formally, the firm's COO began developing a foundation of background information to enable firm leadership to develop an externally focused strategic plan. That background included preparation and augmentation of extensive benchmarking survey data. In addition, the COO prepared extensive trend line analyses on key financial metrics prior to launching the planning process.

The firm's executive committee – together with the CEO and COO – was charged by the members with developing the strategic plan. However, there was mutual understanding that member input would be valuable on the front end of the process. Further, there was universal agreement that key to success at the end of the process would be getting the members on board in supporting the strategic plan.

Fact gathering and background analysis

With benchmarking and financial trend data already in hand, three additional fact gathering steps were pursued in parallel. First, input from members regarding the firm's strengths and weaknesses, external opportunities and threats, potential strategies, and major strategic issues were gathered through two methods. Roughly 20 members were interviewed one-on-one by an independent consultant. Those interviews targeted members with varied perspectives on the firm's development – a group that represented roughly one-third of all members. In addition, all members (equity and non-equity) were invited to complete a survey that covered similar questions. The survey was short and to the point.

Targeted client feedback was gathered in parallel by the consultant. That client input specifically focused on input that could have a direct impact on the strategic planning process (e.g. firm strengths and weaknesses, issues driving the use of Clark Hill and other outside advisors, recommendations for firm strategy, etc.). Client interviews were conducted by telephone. The interviews were structured (i.e. they followed a structured interview guide), but allowed for open-ended dialog with clients.

The client and the member input were integrated with other background information available to Clark Hill. That other information included PWC benchmarking data; Clark Hill financials over multiple years (including member performance statistics); documentation of the direction agreed upon at the firm's fall retreat (i.e. the direction that served as impetus to the strategic planning process); and firm marketing materials.

Ultimately, all background information and analyses were documented and integrated in a foundation report for strategic planning. That report included a SWOT analysis (strengths, weaknesses, opportunities, threats); a summary of the major strategic issues Clark Hill needed to address in the context of its strategic plan; and client feedback. In addition to the integrated report covering the SWOT analysis, client feedback and strategic issues, extensive appendices were provided to the executive committee, including the detailed results of the member survey, more detail from the client feedback interviews, and more detailed tables and schedules covering financial trends and competitive benchmarks.

Strategic planning

The planning process was designed to enable the executive committee to develop a strategic plan in an intensive two-day workshop – building on the extensive background preparation and related discussions outlined in the previous session. The executive committee also began the process with the benefit of knowing the overall direction the members wanted the firm to pursue (e.g. growth to regional leadership and recognition). It should be noted that the executive committee worked two long days, including a working dinner that went well into the evening of the first day.

The workshop began with a review and discussion of the background information and strategic issues. It then focused on affirming and further articulating a strategic direction (based on the overall direction the firm agreed upon the previous fall) – that direction was structured in the form of a vision statement and a related set of primary excellence goals. The executive committee also developed draft strategies for each primary excellence goal (essentially answering the question, "What are we going to do to achieve the goal?"). At the conclusion of the workshop, Clark Hill had a draft one-page strategic plan for the firm.

With a draft strategic plan in hand (a plan that was short of the specifics vis-à-vis how the firm would implement the strategic plan), members of the executive committee gathered feedback and input from their fellow members in small group meetings. That feedback loop proved to be an essential step in building understanding and buy-in – it became a mechanism for accommodating the "committee of the whole" (i.e. involving all equity members directly in strategy development).

Implementation planning

With the member feedback in hand, the executive committee reconvened for a day-long implementation planning workshop. In that one-day workshop the executive committee revised the one-page plan based on the feedback of the members. They managed to make those revisions without watering down the key strategic choices the firm had articulated in the draft plan.

In addition to making strategic plan revisions, the executive committee identified the major initiatives the firm, its practices, and selected members would implement to put the strategy into day-to-day operation. They set priorities among those major initiatives, agreed on organizational adjustments to be made to support the strategy, and agreed on a basic communication plan – both for a planned member retreat and for communication more broadly across the law firm.

Closure and member retreat

Clark Hill used its member retreat to bring the planning process to closure and to formally launch active implementation. One day of the retreat was dedicated to a review of the revised plan and implementation plans; discussion of the implications of the plan (on the firm, the practice groups, and individual attorneys); and informal approval of the plan (subject to any remaining modifications identified at the retreat).

There was very strong agreement with the plan – both on higher level goals and strategies and on more specific action plans. As one indication, the executive committee had included a number of initiatives for practice group level implementation – based primarily on having done portfolio analysis in the strategy development phase. At the retreat, members carried out a similar portfolio analysis in small groups – those small groups reached virtually the same conclusions as the executive committee. That in turn built credibility for the overall plan and the detailed implementation plans that supported it.

Update

We interviewed John Hern, CEO of Clark Hill, to get an update on the firm and its approach to strategic planning and implementation. The following sections provide an update on developments at the firm since the original case study was written in late 2011, subsequent strategic planning processes, and leadership insights on strategic planning.

Developments at the firm

Clark Hill adopted the strategic plan discussed in the case above in fall 2003. Fifteen years later the question is: Did the firm achieve its vision and primary goals? And if the vision was achieved, what came next?

At the time this case study was written, Clark Hill had already more than doubled in size and had expanded both within Michigan and beyond – including building a presence in Chicago and opening a Washington DC office. Roughly a year after this case study was published, Clark Hill merged with Pittsburgh-based Thorp Reed & Armstrong. That merger grew Clark Hill by roughly 50 percent and solidified the firm's regional status. Impressively, a year after the merger, Clark Hill did not lose professional headcount in Pittsburgh – the merger was a genuinely good cultural fit.

With the 2013 merger well integrated, the firm's executive committee (expanded since 2003) revisited the vision (regional growth and recognition) and the primary excellence goals. They also invited all members to revisit the vision and strategy at a member retreat. The members believed that the core focus of the primary goals (which included effective practice group management, individual accountability, unique and positive culture) still worked well as a focal point for strategy and implementation. A "Big Hairy Audacious Goal" (BHAG) (see Collins and Porras, *Built to Last*, 1994, Harper Business Essentials) was adopted, essentially expanding the vision from regional growth to national growth and beyond.

Since that expanded vision was adopted, Clark Hill has continued growing. In 2017 the firm merged with Morris Polich & Purdy, adding nearly 100 attorneys in California and Las Vegas. The following year, Clark Hill merged with Strasburger & Price, adding nearly 200 attorneys and a strong statewide presence in Texas.

Today, Clark Hill is a roughly 650 lawyer firm with 23 offices in the US, plus offices in Dublin, Ireland and Mexico City, Mexico.

Subsequent strategic planning

Clark Hill continued to rest strategic planning (e.g. implementation monitoring, strategic growth management, primary goal setting, etc.) with its executive committee. In parallel, the firm has managed day-to-day implementation – across a growing geographic footprint – through its practice groups.

The executive committee has reaffirmed and refined the primary excellence goals multiple times over the past 15 years. As noted above, the vision and primary goals were revisited by the entire membership after the regional vision had been meaningfully achieved. The broader membership had been well aligned with the strategy over the previous decade via strong practice group integration and management. Thus, when the time came to revisit the vision and primary excellence goals, the membership essentially agreed with the executive committee. The primary goals still worked well for the firm, but the vision needed updating. The firm used the BHAG concept as a tool to frame the question of "What should our new vision be?"

Leadership insights (hindsight is 20/20)

Hern shared a few insights he has gathered regarding strategic planning, strategy implementation, and strategic growth.

- Practice groups can be an extremely effective vehicle for strategy implementation. Clark Hill asks its practice group leaders to think like business unit presidents – and they provide practice group leaders with strong managerial and analytical support to enable disciplined management practices;
- When evaluating strategic growth opportunities (e.g. full scale mergers, as well as additions of lateral groups), cultural fit is a strong predictor of success. As a result, the firm has declined to go forward with mergers that were financial and strategic fits, but not good cultural fits;
- Professional management is a key ingredient to strategic success. Clark Hill's COO has been part of the strategic planning process from the beginning and has been instrumental to both strategy development and strategy implementation. Other professional managers play key roles in post-merger integration, practice group management, talent management and recruiting, and other functional areas; and
- Strategic success requires both a long-term and a short-term orientation. Clark Hill pursued its regional aspirations for close to a decade before agreeing upon a new vision. Yet, it was committed to improving – financial performance, client relationships, professional capabilities, etc. – every day and every year. That combination of continuous improvement and shared vision has proven to be potent.

More information can be found on Clark Hill's website at clarkhill.com.

Case study 3:
Big firm, broad involvement – Bryan Cave Leighton Paisner

Note: This case study was published in winter 2011 – an update on Bryan Cave Leighton Paisner follows this original case study.

Bryan Cave is a global law firm with roughly 1,100 attorneys worldwide. It is among the 25 largest US based firms. In addition, the firm has an international trade consulting affiliate based in Asia, extending the reach of the firm and its ability to add value for companies doing business around the world. Bryan Cave has extensive past experience developing and implementing firm-wide strategic plans.

Initial preparation

When Bryan Cave prepared to revisit and thoroughly rebuild its strategic plan, the firm invested considerable up-front effort in "planning to plan". The firm appointed a large, diverse strategic planning committee (SPC) involving partners from most offices and most practice groups. The SPC included a mix of people with a particular emphasis on younger partners who had not previously had leadership roles. It named a committee chair to act as a formal liaison between Bryan Cave's governing Executive and Management Committees and the ad hoc SPC. The firm's chairman also committed to invest considerable time and effort as a direct participant in the planning process.

The SPC convened prior to the formal launch of the planning process to establish a common framework for strategic planning. The SPC reviewed firm financials and comparisons to an established peer group. They read and discussed background articles covering major trends in the legal industry – with an emphasis on trends affecting major global corporate law firms. The SPC agreed on basic process objectives and parameters for selecting a consultant to assist with planning process management and strategic management advice.

Following the selection of an outside consultant, the SPC agreed on a multi-stage planning process that included a fact gathering and background development phase; a strategic direction setting workshop; a strategy development phase; implementation planning; and plan communication and roll-out. In addition, the SPC committed themselves to maintaining a high level of interaction with and transparency to the broader partnership throughout the planning process.

Fact gathering and background development

Bryan Cave and the SPC were committed to ensuring the strategic planning process was both fact-based and inclusive. The SPC convened to revisit the baseline information it had in hand and agree on additional information to be gathered and analyzed. In addition, the SPC agreed on a two-step approach for gathering input from attorneys across the firm.

Input was first collected qualitatively via in-depth interviews with partners, senior administrators, and associates. Those interviews mixed one-on-one conversations with structured focus groups, providing rich input from attorneys in most of the firm's larger offices. Those interviews were augmented by telephone interviews with partners and others representing the firm's smaller offices.

That qualitative input was translated into a structured questionnaire to provide an opportunity for all of the firm's attorneys to provide input into the planning process. The survey was hosted online, providing a secure and anonymous platform for input gathering. The online design enabled partners to provide additional input on a structured basis on a range of trade-offs that could best be addressed by those who own the firm (in addition to serving clients, managing people, etc.). Survey results provided a statistical assessment of people's views regarding the current state of the firm, the external marketplace, and the future.

Other analyses provided substantial factual grounding, which helped to confirm (in most cases) or challenge (in a few instances) the input provided by attorneys and others via interviews and the structured online survey. Those other analyses included:

- Analysis of financial trends and comparison of financial metrics with peer firms;
- Development of case studies contrasting the apparent strategies and performance of selected global firms (with an emphasis on highlighting the results other firms had achieved from the pursuit of strategies reflective of the alternatives open to Bryan Cave);
- A review and assessment of factors driving various "leading law firm" rankings (e.g. best places to work rankings, the "A-List,"

associate satisfaction surveys, Chambers and other third party rating services, etc.); and

- Structured client input gathered via interviews with a cross-section of clients, including some of the firm's largest, long standing relationships.

Background information and analyses were provided to the SPC (and all partners) in a written report in preparation for a direction setting workshop. The SPC wanted to make sure the focus of the process and the plan was "external", reflecting an understanding of markets, trends, and client needs. The SPC distributed to all partners a series of background pieces prepared by the consultants to educate partners on "macro" issues – and an intranet site dedicated to strategic planning related communications was created early in the process.

Direction setting workshop

The SPC convened for a two-plus day workshop to develop consensus on a strategic direction for Bryan Cave over the next five years. That workshop included substantial time dedicated to discussing the implications of the extensive background analysis that had been developed in the prior phase. That discussion of implications included a listing of the major strategic issues to be addressed in the context of Bryan Cave's strategic plan, and high level strategic alternatives for the firm's future.

The SPC worked primarily as a committee of the whole. However, on several occasions over the course of the workshop, the SPC split into break-out groups to work on elements of the firm's draft strategic direction. By the conclusion of the workshop, the SPC had agreed upon a draft strategic direction that included a mission statement and a set of strategic imperatives (Bryan Cave's version of primary excellence goals, as described earlier in this book).

The **mission statement**, or overall statement of strategic direction, included three elements. First, it expressed a short, easily understood vision focused on being the best global firm at building and sustaining strong and enduring client relationships. Second, it expressed an overall strategy or purpose to drive dynamic change over the life of the strategic plan. And third, it encapsulated the core values of Bryan Cave:

- We are One Firm;
- We have a passionate, long term commitment to our clients;

- We treat our colleagues as we do our best clients;
- We demand and offer professional excellence;
- We promote and embrace diversity; and
- We make a difference in our communities and society.

The **strategic imperatives**, or major goals, covered five areas of focus – a set of goals that are mutually supportive and well aligned. Those imperatives included considerations ranging from strategic growth to financial performance, from people development to (centrally) client relationships.

Wharton Insights

The SPC and the planning process benefited directly from a bit of serendipity. At the time of the strategic planning process, Bryan Cave had a standing leadership development relationship with the Wharton Business School at the University of Pennsylvania. As it so happened, a number of SPC members were scheduled to participate in a leadership-in-residence management development program at Wharton between the strategic direction setting and strategy development phases of the planning process.

The Wharton program was not designed or intended to directly feed Bryan Cave's strategic planning process. However, the executive development program did help crystalize an important strength and competitive advantage Bryan Cave enjoys – an insight that was subsequently shared and discussed extensively within the SPC. Essentially, the Wharton program underscored how and why Bryan Cave could derive sustainable competitive advantage via an ongoing commitment to the vision and strategic direction it already had in draft form.

Strategy development

Bryan Cave's strategy development phase focused directly on identifying and highlighting the trade-offs the firm intended to make in order to achieve each of the strategic imperatives the SPC had developed in the prior phase. Those trade-offs were expressed as action oriented strategies that made **resource priorities** abundantly clear.

At the conclusion of the strategy development phase, the SPC had a very solid draft strategic plan that could be summarized on one page. That one-page plan included:

- A column (or box) that succinctly expressed the vision, overall strategy, and core values;

- A column (captured in five boxes) that captured the strategic imperatives; and
- A column (with boxes flowing directly from each strategic imperative) summarizing the resource priorities Bryan Cave will pursue to achieve the positions implied by each strategic imperative.

Exposure, feedback and refinement

Because Bryan Cave and the SPC were committed from the outset to inclusion and transparency, the draft plan was shared broadly with partners across the firm prior to any implementation planning or formal roll-out and adoption. The chair of SPC and other members of the committee visited every office of the firm to hold meetings with Bryan Cave's partners.

Those meetings included presentation of the draft one-page strategic plan, the background information that influenced the development of that plan, and the logical implications arising from implementation of the plan. The meetings were conversational and provided a platform for feedback, questions, and further refinement of the draft plan.

Implementation planning

With widespread feedback gathered from around the firm, the SPC divided into smaller groups or subcommittees (one for each strategic imperative and related set of resource priorities) to accomplish two tasks. First, the subcommittees integrated partner feedback into the plan, refining selected aspects of that plan based on thoughtful partner input.

Second, the subcommittees developed near term (100 day to one year) implementation initiatives for each strategic imperative. The subcommittees initially developed long lists of potential (logical) implementation initiatives. Those long lists were subjected to a prioritization mechanism similar to the one described earlier in this report. Importantly, the subcommittees applied a degree of pragmatism to implementation prioritization – ensuring the firm did not over-commit resources out of the gate and ensuring that there would be early success through the pursuit of "low-hanging fruit".

The subcommittee chairs worked with the SPC chair to sort out priorities across the five strategic imperatives. This provided an opportunity to eliminate a few points of redundancy (i.e. where more than one group prioritized the same or similar ideas). Implementation plans included action items for the first 100 days of implementation; action items for the first year; and related metrics to facilitate a balanced scorecard approach to implementation management. With that, the formal planning process was complete and the strategic plan and related implementation priorities were ready to be communicated widely across Bryan Cave.

Adoption and formal roll-out

As a large, global law firm, Bryan Cave had the distinct advantage of having highly professional communications capabilities to support strategic plan communications and roll-out. Ultimately, roll-out and communication involved multiple media: a web cast to introduce the plan in advance of face-to-face town-hall meetings; town-hall style meetings at which the plan could be presented and discussed with lawyers and staff; follow-up discussions with practice groups, operating units, and departments; a written document and other print-based communications for reference purposes; an intranet site to provide a continuing hub for strategic plan related communications, updates and feedback; and regular updates and reports from the firm's chairman and from the SPC after implementation formally commenced. Note that roll-out and communication was directed to everyone in the firm – lawyers and staff. The SPC and firm leadership believe everyone in the firm has a role in successful implementation.

A final observation – the strategic plan was designed to be directional in nature. That direction enabled the plan to "cascade" to office level, client service team level, and operating unit level plans. Further, the plan was structured so that resource priorities and strategic imperatives could be recalibrated periodically as the market and economy evolved (something that worked particularly well in light of the global economic downturn).

Update

Since this case study was originally published, Bryan Cave has become Bryan Cave Leighton Paisner (BCLP), following a merger of Bryan Cave with Berwin Leighton Paisner. As noted in the firm's news release announcing the merger:

> *"The merger brings together two organizations widely recognized for their innovative approaches to client service into one global, fully integrated law firm. Bryan Cave Leighton Paisner will provide clients with access to international practice and sector teams in 32 offices across 11 countries and a platform of more than 1,400 lawyers."*

We interviewed BCLP's global co-chair, Therese D. Pritchard, and the chair of the 2007 Strategic Planning Committee, Kenneth L. Henderson, to get an update on the firm and its approach to strategic planning. The following sections provide an update on developments at the firm since the 2007 strategic plan was adopted, subsequent strategic planning processes, and leadership insights on strategic planning.

Developments at the firm

Bryan Cave adopted a strategic plan in 2007. A reasonable question ten or so years later is: did the firm achieve what it identified as strategic priorities and goals? The overall strategy could be summarized as calling for international and domestic growth, a focus on relationships (a source of differentiation), and competitive financial performance.

Developments between adoption of the 2007 plan and development of a new strategic plan in 2014 showed substantial progress in achieving that overall strategy:

- Financial performance improved substantially over that period (both gross revenues and profits per partner); and
- Substantial strategic growth occurred, including:
  - Opened a San Francisco office in 2008;
  - Opened a Paris office in 2008;
  - Merged with Atlanta-based Powell Goldstein in 2009 (a regional leader in the southeast US);
  - Opened a Frankfurt office in 2012; and
  - Merged with Denver-based Holme Roberts and Owen in 2012 (a regional leader in the inter-mountain western US).

The 2014 strategic plan called for international growth (more on that process and its outcomes later). In 2018, Bryan Cave merged with Berwin Leighton Paisner, creating a global firm with offices in 11 countries and 1,400 lawyers. The new firm is among the 50 largest law firms in the world, with co-chairs on two continents.

Subsequent strategic planning processes

Bryan Cave embarked on a large-scale strategic planning process in 2014. That process involved a large and diverse group of partners (similar to the 2007 process). The firm again worked with an outside consultant to help with analytical and process facilitation tasks – but elected to work with a consultant who did not specialize in law firm management. The end product was similar to the 2007 strategic plan, but is a distinctively new plan and strategy.

The mission (vision, purpose, and values) evolved, but remain consistent directionally. The firm intends to be a "first choice" for leading global corporations. It remains committed to growth domestically and internationally (thus, the transformational merger with Berwin Leighton Paisner). And, there were refinements and additions to the list of values.

A new set of primary goals were articulated (three "pillars" for focus – areas that differentiate the firm). In addition to a continued focus on depth and breadth of global client relationships, the firm adopted two new areas of focus. First, the firm decided to more fully leverage an area of strength relative to process and technology innovation, making that an area of focus. Second, the firm agreed to demonstrate thought leadership and build depth of expertise in target practice areas and industries.

The 2014 strategic plan also identified three industry sectors where the firm already enjoyed leading positions. Those industries have become a focal point for thought leadership as well as resource allocation. Further, they have provided a focal point around which practice groups can coordinate on a global basis.

In 2017/18, leaders from Bryan Cave and Berwin Leighton Paisner engaged in a mini-strategic planning process as one means for evaluating the potential for a combined firm (i.e. would the new firm have a compelling strategy that amounted to more than 1+1?). That process was accelerated (roughly two days) and involved small groups from each legacy firm. They developed a shared vision for a combined firm, evaluated the numbers, and identified the synergies the combined firm could exploit. That process was integral in determining that combining forces would be a strategic winner.

Leadership insights (hindsight is 20/20)

Prichard and Henderson shared a few insights they have gathered, having been involved in multiple strategic planning processes:

- Smaller planning teams tend to be more willing to make tough choices (e.g. areas of practice emphasis, industry focus, etc.);
- The strategic plan must identify differentiators for the firm – areas where the firm can achieve genuine leadership and depth;

- It is good to get leaders and strategic thinkers together in a larger scale process to talk about the future of the firm and to get "buy-in" to strategic direction. However, the results of those larger group discussions tend to be "squishy". Not everyone enjoys engaging in that kind of process; and
- Ultimately, a firm needs to have, and try to implement, an agreed upon strategy, or the firm and its practice groups will drift.

More information on the firm is available on the firm's website: www.bryancave.com.